MW01622018

LETTERS TO A DOUBTER

LETTERS TO A DOUBTER

Paul Claudel

Translated from the French by
Henry Longan Stuart

CLUNY
Providence, Rhode Island

CLUNY MEDIA EDITION, 2023

This Cluny edition is a republication of *Letters to a Doubter*,
originally published by Albert & Charles Boni in 1927.

For more information regarding this title
or any other Cluny Media publication,
please write to info@clunymedia.com, or to
Cluny Media, P.O. Box 1664, Providence, RI 02901

VISIT US ONLINE AT WWW.CLUNYMEDIA.COM

ISBN: 978-1685952266

Cover design by Clarke & Clarke
Cover image: Vincent van Gogh, *Flowering Plum Tree (After Hiroshige)*, 1887, oil on canvas
Courtesy of Wikimedia Commons

INTRODUCTION

Happy the man to whom the Lord hath not imputed sin, and in whose spirit there is no guile. (PSALM 32)

Jacques Rivière was twenty years old when he made up his mind to write to Paul Claudel, whom for a year he had admired passionately, and to ask from him some remedy for his disquiet, an answer to the greatest of all questions—in short, to beseech his help in finding God again.

This God was no stranger to him. "He had been brought up in the closest intimacy with Him: he had been taught to rely upon Him in every conjuncture of life, to pray to Him, to follow His counsels, to welcome His inspirations."[1] But his mother had died when he was only ten years old. The stresses and fervors of youth, disgust for the smugness of bourgeois Christianity, the pride of a great intellect, had conspired to conceal God's image from his eyes.

The very desperation of his appeals, whose youthful extravagance reminds us that he was only twenty years old at the time they

1. *Florence* (1924). A novel never completed nor published.

were made, is a burning proof how unable was Jacques to support this deprivation. He had "never succeeded in living without God, nor even at a distance from Him."[2] To all this ardor and commotion Claudel responds with a direct and tireless force, that seems impatient at times only by reason of its confidence, reiterating the unanswerable arguments that Jacques at first refuses to accept.

None the less they enter his soul. There they will never cease to abide until a day comes when, illumined as with sudden light, they take on full life and significance. "This is another saying of Claudel's," Jacques will write in 1915, "which is bearing fruit after all these years."[3]

In 1908, Jacques became engaged. From now on, for all our early confidence that in ourselves we should find a solution of every problem and consolation for every trouble, two were seeking God and praying to Him, evening after evening, for light. For Jacques, Claudel was to remain the friend who is ever at hand when needed. Like a father with a loved child, he scolds and encourages him by turns, not hesitating to oppose him violently when he perceives him entering upon that perilous path of literature, along which Jacques felt that his invincible honesty, the transparent sincerity of the man who could write, "I never lie,"[4] authorized him to advance fearlessly. At every step he takes, Claudel extends a helping hand. It is his kindly interest that procures a professorate at the college Stanislas for the gallant youth who has not suffered lack of means to deter him from the great adventures of marriage and fatherhood.

2. *Florence* (1924).
3. *À la trace de Dieu*, p. 253.
4. *Huitième Carnet de Captivité.*

Little by little, insensibly almost, Jacques advances towards God. With him, there can be no question of sudden conversion. As he himself has put it, "Conversion means simply turning oneself in the right direction."[5] And he has never left the road of Christianity. For a long time, he may have walked along it with closed eyes. Nevertheless, even at the period when he most obstinately refused to call himself a Christian, he has always been, in the full force and beauty of the term, the "man of good will," by whom no burden was shirked, whom no danger ever frightened, who always did his best with the means given him, who accepted happiness and suffering, success and frustration, with the same docile and loving heart, and with whom whatever God did was always for the best. Perhaps his strongest objection to Catholicism had lain in the fear that, by facilitating his life and showing him its every problem illumined in advance, it might very well deprive him of his favorite task of investigation, for which the term "taking to pieces" is hardly too strong, and of that reconstruction from its own elements to which he subjected every work, every event, and every creature, and which was the passion of his life.

Apart altogether from the counsels of Claudel, and slowly instructed by life itself, he was bound to perceive that the way which leads to God is no easy or sunny one. On the contrary, it is a road piled with rocks, choked with thorns, marked by many a humiliating fall, the more difficult to recognize and to follow the further along it that one advances—a road, in short, that each wayfarer must make for himself, because for every wayfarer it must be hewn manfully and breast-high through a very jungle of obstacles. Thank

---

5. *À la trace de Dieu*, p. 47.

God, at the end of every path, a light shines! For some it is dazzling. For others, alas, small and dim, it too often vanishes from sight as the way turns and twists. Nevertheless for him who has once perceived it, even at the darkest and most desperate moment there remains the assurance that he will see it again, the knowledge that his efforts are made not in vain, that he is advancing towards it and that, where it shines, the Sovereign Good, the Supreme Truth, awaits him.

Freed little by little of this extraordinary terror he had of over-ease, and finding no obstacle worthy his consideration still before him, Jacques yields. At Christmas, 1913, without great enthusiasm or any strong assurance that his darkness has been dispersed—in short, "by an act with which a noble deliberation of judgment had much more to do than the demands of sentiment,"[6] he asks from Heaven the spiritual food whose benefit he is not to feel until a few months later[7] when the hazard of disaster has really "cast him upon God."[8]

It was during the three years spent as a prisoner of war, that the good seed sown by Claudel took root, swelled and bore fruit a hundred-fold. Read *À la trace de Dieu* and you will find an answer to all the questions posed in the *Correspondence.* Here are certitude and light after so much doubt and so much darkness, here is the presence of God, here is His visible hand, supporting, invigorating Jacques, defending him, keeping him, as it were, afloat on this ocean of somber suffering, and choosing the moment of bodily and mental misery, when the very soul seemed exhausted from its

6. Preface by Paul Claudel to *A La Trace de Dieu*, p. 24.
7. Ibid.
8. *À la trace de Dieu*, p. 210.

dreary oscillations in the void, to instill that joy which none may taste save through deprivation and the surrender of everything that is not itself.

How, it might well be asked here, could Jacques ever disown a faith so firmly held—reject a God whom he had seen at his side for three years—voluntarily avert his eyes from a light that had been so mercifully compassionate?

For the very reason that, in the interminable solitude of his prison, a habit of silence had grown upon him, which he was never able to break. Through the sheer necessity of explaining himself to himself and to no other, he had lost the taste, and perhaps the faculty, for showing the inwardness of his beliefs to anyone on earth, save indeed to a single soul, whose place was at the core of his own and of which he has written: "It is one with me." Because he did not speak of God after the war, it has been too readily concluded that God was forgotten.

Certainly, outside evidence lent color to this belief. The gush of love which had produced *À la trace de Dieu* seemed sunk in its socket, the flame which still glowed under the ashes, to be quenched. Even within (the fact must be faced) there reigned silence and reserve.

The reasons for this silence, for this aridity, for the undeniable subsidence of love for God in Jacques, are of a twofold order. Some were exterior and even material. Others are to be sought in the nature of the man, perhaps—if we may dare speculate upon what necessarily surpasses our feeble understanding—in the very designs of God on his behalf.

Hardly had he escaped from the hell of imprisonment when he found himself gripped, fettered and stifled by material necessity.

There was no time now to speak of his heart or feelings.[9] The problem was one of daily bread. A terrible physical fatigue descended upon him, the natural reaction to three years of nervous tension. For three more years he was practically using up his reserves of strength in order to accomplish his task. In danger at any moment of breaking down under the growing burden of work, difficulties, and lack of capital, he was fighting down his weakness with a desperate courage that finally prevailed. Throughout this period the problem of gaining a livelihood for himself and those dear to him, together with his work upon the *Nouvelle Revue Française*, to which he gave new life, absorbed all his energies. Just as we defer writing to some best-beloved indefinitely, because we feel the letter is too vital a one to be written amid distractions, so Jacques put off speaking of God. Everything he did was done conscientiously. He was incapable of giving himself by halves. "That tepidity towards God which began to disturb me," he tells us, "also meant that I was losing the habit of attention."[10] So long as a thousand preoccupations, a thousand duties, demanded this attention, how could he undertake a task which he desired final and triumphal, how dare to place at the service of God a being so dispersed?

Does this mean that he had ceased to think of God, that he rejected Him? Far from it. Never once had he desired to hide himself from God's face. Never, to the last day of his life, did he omit that evening prayer in which the Christian confesses his misery, owns his dependence, and begs for assistance. It is true that towards the end, he gave up attendance at Mass almost completely. But, in the

9. *Aimée* as well as *À la trace de Dieu* were entirely written during his imprisonment.
10. *Cinquième Carnet*, p. 60.

first place, early rising had become a physical impossibility. In the second, late mass, as it is celebrated in our bigger churches, by some anonymous priest, in the midst of a ceaseless come-and-go, shuffling of chairs and clink of *sous*, was a positive torture, something in which he could not find God. His scrupulous faith demanded some measure of silence and recollection. And, with that hatred of anything less than perfect which was at once his virtue and his handicap, he preferred disobedience to obeying so ill.

It is also true that he refused to own himself a Catholic publicly, to enroll himself under any banner—to march in any processional ranks. Why? Through humility—but also through pride.

Humility! With his mind always fixed on what remained to be done, and oblivious of what he had accomplished—comparing himself always with the Creator and never with the creature, Jacques remained conscious of his faults and imperfections, but never of his virtues. He could never conceive of salvation as easy. He knew that if he were on the road it was to get somewhere. Looking back towards his point of departure he never told himself complacently: "See how far I have come! I am a Christian now!" Rather he looked toward the goal and cried: "My God, how shall I ever reach You?"

He knew, too, that until the day of our death, when He takes us at last to His bosom, God is never caught up with. He walks ahead of us forever and to halt on the road is to risk seeing Him pass from our sight.

His pride! It told him that, in the daily progress toward God, he was not of those who follow, but of those who are followed. He was fully conscious that he was re-opening a route long abandoned and that it was for others to march behind. "My God," he cries, "you have thrown me among my brethren, perhaps in order that, in returning to you I may not return alone, but bring you those of whom I am a fellow-captive."[11] He refuses to stay his voyage of discovery or to cast anchor in some sheltered port with all these *arrivés*, so sure of themselves and of their accomplished virtue. He is unwilling to accept any God circumscribed, fashioned or delimitated by the measure of our petty hemisphere. He wants to push his investigation beyond any limits hitherto traced. Using the gift of penetration which he has received, it is his intention, he tells us with a naïve assurance, "to explore the psychology of God." He would advance, discover, fill in blank spaces upon the incomplete chart—gain for human knowledge new territories of the Divine.

He believed that his vocation called upon him to strive to understand not only God, but everything that lived, that thought, or spoke around him. All our possessions, he felt, are lent us by God, and must one day be restored unimpaired to His hands. The first duty then is to discover what is the proper place of each one in that divine hierarchy of which the exercise of our feeble reason gives us only some vague hint.

> All that mass of thought, forever in turmoil, like waters at their source, how shall I understand, and not take part?
>
> All that mass of sound, forever becoming speech. Perhaps, after all, something interesting is being said. Who is to interpret if I stand aside?[12]

11. *À la trace de Dieu*, p. 312.
12. Paul Claudel, *Feuilles de Saints, Jacques Rivière*, p. 196.

Knowledge, for him, meant love. "Never has anything passed before me without affecting me strongly, or left me without taking away with it as it went something of my love and of my life."[13] To this second task he gave himself up with such fervor that one might be excused for believing he found it all sufficient and that in neglecting the first he had forgotten the Master who assigned him both one and the other. Like an entomologist who holds his breath for fear of disturbing the frail insect he is studying, he imposed silence upon himself. Henceforth he would neither intervene nor judge. He will reject (and with how infallible a gesture!) all that is false or counterfeit. But everything that bears the mark of authenticity, good and evil alike, is to have a right to his patient investigation. That extraordinary prayer, in which all the apparent obscurities of his conduct are made clear, came from his heart in all sincerity and in all simplicity: "My God, create within me an intelligence that is unencumbered, pure and candid, wherein I may receive the ideas of others. Grant that I may never seek to substitute for these any ideas of my own, save those only which Thou shalt prescribe me for their good."[14]

Conscious that he is living in an hour, not so much of correction, as of fuller understanding, he has all the air of setting morality aside. And yet this very morality, rejected as an instrument for his work, was never once repudiated by him as a guide, nor offended by the slightest gesture of his life. He could not, even though he would, have liberated himself from its control. It was something stronger even than he. He was honest as some men are dark-haired or snub-nosed, by birth and without the remotest prospect of change. To

---

13. *Correspondance*, p. 183.
14. *Huitième Carnet*, p. 67.

lie, to deceive, were for him such sheer impossibilities that the contempt in which he held them was almost childish in its naïveté. He regarded them more as limitations of character than as sources of power. Later on, when the unfinished novel which his last wishes withhold for the present, is published, no one will find it the perverse book which a few misunderstood phrases that escaped from his pen, have led certain persons to expect. Instead we shall see how, when fleshly love is his theme, even with the aid of what associations he could gather from his own instincts to lend realism to his hero, he was forced to remain chaste; that, in all the force of the phrase, evil was a closed book to him. In his innocence of heart he even believed that such was the case with the rest of the world. He thought that everyone possessed an armor like his own, against which evil only blunted its barb and wasted its poison. If he did not fear evil it was because he was skeptical of its power. If he neither could nor would condemn, it was because he had never had an adequate vision of human malice. Full of insight where the world of thought was in question, he was a myopic face to face with human action. He believed that when others spoke of their sins, they, like himself, were referring to their temptations!

Does this mean that he was unaware of the difference between good and evil, and for this reason refused ever to sit in judgment? None will so believe after reading this conclusion to a long debate, in the last of his lectures: "There is no question here of refusing to pass judgment. It is in order to reach a safer one that we must have patience awhile." What man who loved disorder or evil could write, two months before his death, in a sort of unconscious résumé of his life and life-work, and as though stirred by the obscure premonition of an hour close at hand when God would judge both:

> The soil is taking me back. I shall end by having an intelligence as orderly as a vineyard.
>
> Do you believe that there has been no combat? No! I have felt—I still feel—immense solicitations to evil.
>
> But everyone must choose. I have chosen. I choose to be safe.
>
> Thus I range myself with creatures of a category I detest, which I find irksome and insupportable. People who will have to be suppressed unless we wish to see a reign, already so powerful and so widely extended, established upon earth—the reign of the lie.[15]

Morality, however, is not God. Even if Jacques remained faithful to the former, did he keep his faith in the latter?

Necessarily, he must have, since he complains of being "abandoned."[16] Herein indeed lay the punishment of his pride. He refuses the Divine assistance, and it will not be given him in his own despite. God will suffer him to fight alone. Since his task absorbs him to such a degree that he is no longer able to raise his eyes to God—since he gives himself to it so thoroughly that he has no longer time to give God anything, God will leave him the task as sole recompense. "I feel," he had once written, "that if I gave myself more I should be better received."[17] Now, since he is giving himself less, God receives him no longer, withdraws from him His presence and His ear. As a result there is a sensible diminution of succour and of

15. *Second lecture on The Relations between Literature and Morals*, given at Geneva, December 9, 1924.
16. Letter to François Mauriac.
17. *À la trace de Dieu*, p. 217.

joy. But not of faith. Upon grace a long sleep descends. The love of God grows numb. But the need of God persists. Who, in the case of the most heartfelt affections, has not experienced these sudden silences, wherein everything seems to die away, except the need of loving?

Moreover, by one of those marvelous dispensations of God at which Jacques, throughout his writings, has never ceased to marvel, that very penance and privation which he inflicts upon himself is destined to redouble the force of his influence in the future, and to become, one might say, the very medium of his message.

For consider a moment the circle by which Jacques is surrounded, those "brothers" of whom he is in his own words "the fellow captive." Suppose that he had, from the date of his return to France, proclaimed himself a Christian. Upon what authority could he have relied to impose his ideals? Who would have followed this young man, undecided and unsettled as he then appeared? Before the habit of confidence in his judgment could be acquired by these disciples, certain things were indispensable. First, a free access to that "unencumbered and intact" intelligence for which he had prayed. Then the knowledge, gained by seeing him at his steadfast work, that his judgment was to be trusted, precisely because he weighed every element, kept nothing back, and showed only what he himself had seen, because he never lied, did not even know how to set about invention, and because his honesty was flawless. Little by little, the authority which he used so modestly, and whose full force was not felt until after his death, has to be acquired. He has to become "the man at the helm,"[18] the pilot who "knows what he

18. Joseph Delteil, *Nouvelle Revue Française* (April 1, 1925), p. 541.

is doing and whither he is bound,"[19] before some at least surrender themselves so completely to his direction that on the day the message which he kept hidden for them in his heart strikes them with its full force, they will be unable to restrain their fervor and will be precipitated "into the bosom of truth itself."[20]

Had he waited overlong to deliver that message? Was his task beginning so utterly to absorb him that there was danger of his forgetting its purpose and walking disarmed into danger? Or was it because God judged that the effort had been enough and the recompense earned that the decree went forth which took him so untimely from the number of the living?

In either case, Jacques knew that his hour had come. He accepted his sentence. For months, behind the joy in sheer living which never shone from him so radiantly, a hand that was hidden but very powerful was detaching him little by little from life. There were times when a flash of lightning seemed to pierce the darkness that covered the unknown road, and when he realised whither he was being led. "I do not understand why it is," he would say suddenly, "but I feel barely alive." At other times, instead of surprise, there was resignation. "I assure you, I am no longer attached to life. Were it not for you and the children, I could die without a pang." Stricken to the heart, I would ask him what he was trying to tell me. But the curtain had fallen again. He could not recall what had been in his mind to say. The anxiety no longer oppressed him which, for years, had led him continually to repeat: "I have five years, perhaps ten, to live. Do you think I shall have time to finish all I want to do?"

19. Paul Claudel, *Correspondance*, p. 69.
20. *À la trace de Dieu*, p. 183.

Resistance was at an end. In the midst of the daily projects with which his brain still swarmed, he knew the task was over. In "an abyss of sadness, resignation and courage,"[21] he took up the last and supreme effort where he had laid it down. From now on he had no care save how to "despoil himself, becoming dry and bare and poor, as death should find a man."

There was no trace of revolt when death came. He fought for life bravely, just as in every other eventuality he had done whatever there was to do, and as well as it might be done. Earthly hope there was none. "I have been dead," he told us, "for several months." Soon his mind was absorbed entirely by the other world. He called for his mother—for the beloved friend who had passed over before him.[22] "Henri, I am coming!" At last the sombre struggle, so bravely borne, was over. The era of doubts and contentions was at an end and the realm of light attained. "Look! The gates are opening," he cried. "I am going to find the divine light."

As the Holy Oils anointed those eyes, closed already to the world, with what overwhelming and all-merciful splendor must that light have steeped his soul to draw from a Christian who had ever deemed himself an unworthy and unprofitable servant, the great cry of triumph and thanksgiving which he has left behind him as the key to the heavenly dwelling where he waits our coming: "Now I am saved—by a miracle!"

Isabelle Rivière

21. *À la trace de Dieu*, p. 272.
22. Henri Alain-Fournier.

LETTERS TO A DOUBTER

CORRESPONDENCE

(1907–1914)

To Paul Claudel

BORDEAUX, 14TH FEBRUARY, 1907

For more than a year I have been living by you and in you: my faith, my perpetual preoccupation, all this you have been to me. I have adored you as Cebès adored Simon: I have prostrated myself before you, I have reached supplicating hands towards your soul. But what I want from you is a different certitude, some answer other than that which you have given in *Tête d'Or*. This is why, after long deliberation, I have made up my mind to write you. And oh, my young elder brother—you in whom I have grown so to confide—this answer, that shall put an end to my doubts, I desire so ardently! Be brutal to me if you will, fling me to the ground, insult me, but give me my answer!

Here am I! Twenty years old, very much like the rest of the world, without any special happiness or unhappiness, but with a restlessness, oh, a terrible restlessness, that dates back to the beginning of my life, that by turns uplifts me and refuses me all satisfaction, a restlessness which plunges me alternately in transports of delight and transports of despair, a restlessness quite untiring!

I have flown to books. Some have delighted me, I have believed in them, loved them like so many older and wiser brothers. Yet, each time, this restlessness has warned me that I must not rest, that I must not be satisfied, that what I love must be destroyed, that I must go on, suffering, seeking, panting. Like every other young man, I once believed that failing everything else I might find happiness in my very lack of certainty, permit myself to be cradled in an exquisite disenchantment. Barrés entertained me; I found him delightful. But even in Barrés, what I most admired was his cult of desire. And this, at bottom, is nothing but restlessness. I have desired, and how intensely! One evening, my very soul weary from feeding upon itself, I felt anew the stir of anxiety, the cry from within, the challenge, the revolt—my passion! Then André Gide became my teacher. I went off hunting for *things* and for the happiness which they do not hold; my hands stretched out before me, I sought satisfaction in possessions; recurrent deceptions failed to discourage me. "For every object, no matter what its nature, I could find a frenzied adoration."

> *It is then that you came.*
> *You alone.*
> *… You have been to me victory and visitation.*

For a month I had been awaiting you. Even when I knew nothing of you save your name, I was already the prey of a presentiment. So well indeed was I aware what your work in me would be that I did not dare make up my mind to know you. Then one day I took you up. I read you from end to end, understanding nothing, yet troubled as by a strange anguish. Little by little, and through some secret and marvelous progression, I experienced the germination of your lesson, the full flowering of your revelation. How it happened I do not know, but these took place within me while even yet I did not understand. But oh, the transport of joy when, finally, intelligence reached me, when at last I realized the treasure with which I was filled! For over a year now, its development has gone on. It is from you that, like a child, I have learnt everything. Each day has brought me some new certitude; your voice has penetrated every fibre of my spiritual being, I have caught your very habits of thought. Today the invasion is complete. To command me you have only to think; my very life has been renewed by yours. Secretly I have given you names—brother, and resurrection, and beatitude—him by whom the way and the truth is taught me. During the night I have wakened from dreams of you—as if you had not been at my side! And this for a year…!

I questioned myself. By whom, I asked, are you given this admirable serenity, this strength and certitude, this confidence, this joy? And at last I understand. I know that God is helping you and that you live in God. But then—but then—the old cry, the old disquiet that you had stilled in me woke anew. Today the ancient revolt is back. Again I feel my anguish assail me. And I have resolved to ask of you—Peace!

Yes, Peace! Oh, this God, this God! I long so to feel Him present, here, close to me, solid and unmistakable, to be done with seeking Him, to put an end once for all to this dreaming of happiness. And yet, after having been your intimate for so long, I look within myself; I find the old aridity, the same horror, the same distress and nausea. Peace! Give me your answer—and with it—Peace! Show Him to me, make me taste of Him, feel His weight upon my heart:

"Heavy am I and drunken with His presence." I want Him pressed so close to me that I can no longer even tremble.

Now, let me tell you the worst of all my ills—nay, my disease itself. This struggle, this spasm, this revolt, this desire, this restlessness are tearing me to pieces—yet I adore them! Never to be satisfied, to find an answer in nothing—it is these very things that I hug to my soul. Nothing else, in the first place, tore me away from Catholicism. I turned from its spiritual nourishment. I preferred my miserable hunger, my throes of anguish. Now you know my disease. And yet I must seek its cure.

"At least it is mine, at least it is my own." But I know that I must not let dissatisfaction satisfy me, nor erect misery into a god. I yearn for an answer from you—something so sweet that, almost without my knowing how, my misery will dissolve in it; a touch of your hand upon my shoulder—my very own shoulder, that will make all things clear. Somehow it seems to me that no more is needed—just some whispered counsel. But whispered to me, *to me* and to no one else amid created beings. How well I should understand then, how clearly I should see! Don't think that I am asking for explanation, or for anything like an exegesis. No. What I beg is nothing more than a gesture, your head bowed in assent—the word "yes" formed upon your lips. Cure me, ah, cure me, my brother, dear young elder! Be my resurrection! This is what I have come to!

I must bring this poor letter, turgid and declamatory as it is, to an end. I had intended the sheets I enclose you merely to be a rough draft, but I am going to send them just as they are. I don't want to think over them. If I did, in all probability my detestable vanity would dissuade me from such an appeal. Accept them then—my prayer and cry for help. I shall be waiting for your reply, in such anxiety—such desperate hope. Send it, please, to JACQUES RIVIÈRE, 7 RUE HUSTIN, BORDEAUX.

I write this letter after consulting M. F.—whom I met two months ago and who lent me *Partage de Midi*.

To Paul Claudel
BORDEAUX, 10TH MARCH, 1907

I cannot wait to write till I get your answer. I am stifling and must cry aloud for help. I implore you—do not think the worse of me because I seem to be dramatizing what is an actual torture.

Two things will prevent me from ever being a Christian: my feeling that *nothingness is a reality*, and my contentment with my own despair.

Nothingness! This is what really is poisoning me. I do not, like Besme, have it forever against my face, nor live in a perpetual confrontation with it. Oftenest I do not think of it, am able to ignore it altogether. But there are moments when, suddenly—without any warning, I feel it beside me. I sense its presence and my whole being is upheaved. It is as though something which did not exist said to me, using no words: "Here I am!" Behind all that I see looms this horrible visage of that which has no existence. It is some monster, some formless substance, some presence that I would fain repel yet cannot—*cannot* drive from me. But, oftener still, the evil is more perfidious because so mild—so gentle. The thing seems to happen to me by preference just as I am *about* to let the charm of some quiet landscape invade my soul.

Summer mornings, limpid, astir with life, spangled with immortal renewal.

Winter afternoons. Beyond the river, hidden in its valley, my eye dwells on the dear outlines of the familiar hills.

Dusk of spring evenings. Above the slate slabs of the little courtyard, swallows wheel in the air. On the Place St. Pierre, the children are shouting at their play.

Summer nights. The sun has set. I can hear footsteps on the highway. Stroke by stroke the Angelus melts into the environing silence.

Sundays in late fall. The air is dense, the sky opaque. The great bell from the cathedral is droning over the city.

And always, always, at the very moment when the great solace which you describe in *Octobre* is pouring into my soul, the evil thing is upon me. At first an imperceptible wound, then something whose ravages consume me utterly. A point stabs my heart, a despair infiltrates that is as slender as a thread and as deadly as a sword. My brother, I suffer! My arms fall at my side, I am past even the desire to weep: I am vanquished, I am in the grip of some terrifying sweetness: I feel that what one terms "all this" is vain, has no meaning, leads nowhere—that it exists, in a word, void of all design, goal or desire, and in a fashion so precarious that it scarcely conceals the horrible presence of that other—which is not.

This is my sickness, brother of mine. In a way, it is that of Cebès. In him I once thought I recognized myself, and was hopeful of a remedy. But I have begun to understand that I am past cure, because my disease is deeper rooted, is more irremediable than his. Its most atrocious feature is that I really cherish it, that I make of it my life and unique joy. Down in my heart I would hate not to suffer from it. Cebès sought, questioned, seized the knees of Simon. I too have the air of being a suppliant. But I do not really want to be cured. Horrible thought! I relish my distress, I am passionately in love with my abjection, I embrace my spectre. Can you still understand me? When I cried to you, "An answer!" I was lying. Or rather, if I begged for it, it was only in order that, with a laugh, I might cast it aside, that I might mock your words. Since my last letter, remorse for such duplicity has been stirring in me; it is to make amends for it that I write you now. Realize the full extent of my moral misery! I want to be nursed, but not to be cured. The joy you promise me, I desire to possess only that I may reject it. You have so upheaved me that I begrudge you, and can only know peace after having cast this insult in your face. To punish you for having disquieted me, I want to show you that you don't disquiet me at all. You shall not—*you shall not* destroy the calm of my anguish!

No! For I love that anguish too thoroughly. I have told you that it meant all my life to me. And it is true. Each wound it inflicts absorbs me during an entire day. After having suffered from some country landscape, I am in ecstasy. The joy and sorrow it has given me blend as though in a process that is never completed. To see some tranquil lover of the picturesque taking his ease before a fine sunset, while I am savouring my sudden distress, fills me with a positive transport wherein contempt for my neighbor is mingled. I know that such a joy is vile, puerile and unworthy. But I am unable to deny myself one drop of its gratification.

Now you see, my brother, in what torture I am immersed. Do not believe what I have just told you. I do want to be cured—I do desire peace. But with what entreaties, with what infinite delicacy you will have to give it to me! You have seen the recoil of my miserable pride, you have been shown the extent of my damnation, and now, more desolate than ever, with a still more lamentable cry and suffocating like a drowning man who reaches his hands above the water, I cling to you, I grapple you to me. Oh, free me from all this vileness, from these stupid puerilities. Reveal the pure word which will loosen my tongue: suffer my heart to beat freely, open my ears to the murmur of eternal fountains!

And yet… Again, no! I no longer say, "I don't want to be cured," but I say this: "I shall never be cured, I know I shall never be cured, why I do not know, but I know that I shall never be cured." My separation from Christianity took place amid too much indifference. There is something in me, some imperceptible but profound lassitude, that poisons all my efforts, especially my efforts to believe. It is quite possible that this languor has by now become a vague and latent state of conscience, that this feeling as to the reality of nothingness has turned to a secret but invincible familiarity with *the presence* of nonexistence. I have no hope, but this time I repeat it with grief in my heart and tears in my eyes.

March 17

This time I ought to tell you all my little scruples, all my secondary difficulties. But this I do only for the sake of completeness. I feel that if you could once conquer my indifference, jog my lassitude, give me a real desire for joy and peace, relieve me of this frightful obsession of non-existence, put me in communication with Him who is—I know, I say, that these minor difficulties would disappear.

None the less, I will tell you what they are.

First, are you so sure that you are in possession of the veritable significance of Christianity? I mean, not only the significance that its founders gave it, but that which its representatives preserve today? How many are there who understand Christian dogma in the same sense as yourself? For what pope, for what saint, is the admirable interpretation of it that you offer, the true one? What would it mean if you alone had kept the actual significance of Jesus, and all other Christians had forgotten it? What sort of religion would a religion be that was misunderstood by all the faithful save one? How am I to believe in the divine origin of a dogma, which, in the course of its transmission, has been so indefinitely disfigured?

I know what you will reply. "The Church interprets her doctrine as I do."

If so, for pity's sake, show me this in some detail. Prove to me that for her the Redemption, Hell, Calvary mean the same thing they mean to you.

There is something else. I seem to see Christianity dying. In spite of yourself, even you have uttered a terrible phrase: "No one knows what has happened it."

Indeed, none of us know what has happened it. Nor what to make of those spires above the roofs of our great towns which symbolize no longer the prayer of any of us. Nor the meaning today of those great fabrics, hemmed in by railway stations and hospitals, and from which the people themselves have driven the monks. Nor what those stucco crosses, disfigured by an abominable art, that stand above the graves in our cemeteries, would tell us.

"Their roots are in the heart."

Very little! Pure habit! People have no longer any real care for God, no desire, no memory. Everything is reduced to so many Sunday usages which it would be irksome to change.

Personally, I should be glad to be sure that all this humanitarian socialism is only a passing malady, and not, as I fear, the truth, the imminent reality, the new dogma. You would confer a benefit upon me by proving to me that the roots of dogma survive, that its tendency is to flourish anew, that today it is merely asleep and not in its coma of death.

I fear you will tell me: "Read such and such a saint, who will give you peace." Or else: "Go to confession and communion, grace will be given you and you will believe." I don't want any answer of that sort. It is to you that I am writing—it is you alone who have known how to speak to me. What I am asking from you is not some practical advice, or the recommendation to betake myself to some priest (I don't like priests). Rather a rebuke; but in words so weighty, so true, that I shall experience the definite thrill, the inward recognition of the truth, the discovery of the Real Presence that will mean for me re-admission to existence.

March 23

Here I am, still using big words. And yet, all I say to you is so strongly felt. I want to speak simply, if only to make you realize the sincerity of my uneasiness.

Listen, then! I am writing you on one of the first real spring evenings of the year. The day is sinking peacefully to its close. From some country fair or other, the sound of distant music reaches my ear, to others, perhaps, a simple, melancholy air, yet one that pierces my soul with anguish because it seems like a voice given to futility, an intimate and invincible irony breathing from the landscape beneath my eyes, the very murmur of its nothingness! Look where I will, I find a flaw that ruptures all harmony, some secret fissure through which the whole is shattered. It is from this, and nothing else, that I suffer. And it is in this very suffering that I take such delight.

How could you expect me, with such a malady of the soul, to believe frankly and freely in one terrible Existence! How would you have me ask a cure from faith when my sickness is precisely the impossibility of having any faith in the world's reality! I come back to this again and again, because it seems to me the main thing which prevents me from being a believer. The rest is a trifle.

The habitual form which this sentiment of the vanity underlying everything takes in me, is a sort of aesthetic curiosity, an intangible irony, an imperceptible smile which none guesses when I find myself the host of anything approaching emotion. Not that I play the universal dilettante. That is a pose I execrate. I am not only capable of passion, but of being eaten up—consumed by it. Nevertheless, it is at the very moment emotion has strongest hold of me that I feel most strongly the vanity and nothingness of it all. Without abating my feeling of pleasure for one moment, that smile of which I have just spoken, and in whose presence nothing serious can subsist, forms within me. This is not the whim of a psychologist amusing himself with the mechanism of his own soul. It is the reaction upon my mind of the irrationality, the futility, the general "what's the use" which is upheaving me at this very moment. Apart altogether from the terrible moments when nothingness rears itself before my face as an assailant, I live with it, am conscious of it seated at the very centre of my being! It has become my familiar devil, it infects my life, it renders any sure knowledge of the way I should follow an impossibility.

Just now I have been reading in *Connaissance de l'Est* certain terrible words which might almost be the sentence of my own damnation and which confirm me in the idea that I am irretrievably lost. "From now on, he enters Nirvana. Are people astonished I should use this word? For me the concepts of Nothingness and Enjoyment are closely akin. This is indeed the ultimate and devilish mystery: silence steeping the creature sealed up in his integral refusal, incestuous peace descending upon the soul that is based solidly upon its own essential difference."

At least I have not lost my anxiety, at least I do not rest tranquil in my possession of nothingness. I take no pleasure in nothingness—what I do take pleasure in is the suffering it inflicts on me, and which might be called its antithesis. Deep in my heart I hold to the idea that a disturbed soul is never lost and that salvation may some day reach me through my very anguish.

Before bringing to an end this long letter, in which I have tried to set forth the reasons for my disbelief just as they occurred to me and without any attempt to present them in logical sequence, I must add a word upon two things that I find a hindrance and a stumbling-block: these are my sensuality and my avarice.

I am sensual to this extent. Every natural sensation reaches me with such terrible poignancy that it quite literally beclouds my soul. The beauty of light and darkness, the taste of water, the odors of the soil, and certain indescribable harmonies composed of all these things together, leave me in a fog of voluptuousness. It is as though my body, overcharged by pleasure, were pressing upon my soul and stifling it. These accesses are continuous. I fear they effectively preclude any durable contemplation or that inner fervor which, like the lamp before the altar, should never be let go out. In short, my senses weigh too heavily upon my heart to permit me to watch and pray.

Then, my avarice. I would prefer to be like Violaine, prodigal, spontaneous in giving. But a host of petty scruples deter me from so noble a gesture. I want this or that reservation made clear. I have my own little philosophies to which I am unconsciously attached. I am held back on all sides, incapable of surrendering myself once and for all into His hands who would be my Guide.

Innumerable and detestable fetters! Petty meannesses, all the harder to destroy because so hard to detect! Will you not give me the strength to break away from them all? Will you not give me that impetus Gide could not afford me, turning my face not, as Gide would have persuaded me (and failed), towards material things, but towards God? To leave all these behind, to awake one morning out of their reach forever, how I long for this! And yet I cannot!

Dear brother, I await from you my very life to come!

Jacques Rivière

P. S. My first letter was dashed off in a moment, by a sheer effort of will, and mailed you immediately. I hardly remember now what I said. It must be a hundred times more childish even than this one. Please forget it and judge me by what I have written you in this. Above all, for pity's sake, tell me if my disease is curable, and if so, cure it for me. Above all, eradicate from my heart the hideous joy of self-complacency. (JACQUES RIVIÈRE)

To Jacques Rivière
TIEN-TSIN, 3RD MARCH, 1907

My dear boy,

I had started to write you a long theological letter. Then I felt ashamed of acting the pedant and the professor. Between us two, I see, it is man to man. Therefore I turn towards you, I open my arms and say: Yes, I am willing! Be my brother, come over on my side. Come to God, Who is calling you. I know a moment of terrible anguish lies before you. But—*it must be done.* The very phrase that is made the theme of one of the last quatuors of Beethoven. *Muss es sein?* And in what exultant notes the great musician-soul answers! *Ess muss sein! Ess MUSS sein!* Every conversion, Pascal tells us, is a sentence of doom. There are many things which appear to you infinitely sweet—terribly desirable, which you will have to renounce. On the other hand, in the Catholic religion, there are so many things hard to believe, humiliating to practice. There is such a pitiless abasement of our own little notions, our own little personality! But be brave! *It must be done.* Don't listen to those who tell you that youth is the time for enjoyment. Youth is not formed for pleasure, but for heroism. The word is not too strong. A young man must be a hero today to resist the temptations that surround him, to be the lonely believer in a despised doctrine, to face the arguments, the blasphemy, the scurrility which fill our books, our newspapers, and our streets, without giving way a finger's breadth—to resist his family and his friends, to be one against many, to be faithful against all. Nevertheless, be of good heart. Remember: "I have conquered the world." Don't dream that your sacrifice will diminish you. On the contrary, you will be quite marvelously augmented. It is by and through *virtue* that a man is manly. Chastity will render you vigorous, prompt, alert, acute—clear as a bugle call and resplendent as the sun at its rising. Life will seem to you full of savour and significance, a world of reason as well as of beauty. The further you advance, the more easy will everything become. You will laugh at the obstacles which frown on you now. As for all these poets and writers, these great names that have overshadowed your youth, suddenly the flimsiness and grotesque of all of them will reach you. You will perceive—I do not say the poverty—but the sheer nothingness of the anti-Christian ideology. For there is no science save in unity, there is no dialectic save by the Yes and the No, and he who withdraws the Word destroys speech.

Moreover, you are not alone. Think of the immense crowd of wretched beings, of poor creatures whose hell on earth such terrible books as *Bubu* by Phillippe, or *La Maternelle* by Frapié, describe for us; who live and die in moral darkness and disease, while you have leisure, intelligence, and instruction. It is for you to be the delegate of light to all these beings of the abyss. What answer, think you, will you make to them when they accuse you before God, and ask you: "What have *you* done with all your gifts?" Woe to you then if you have only used these gifts to make their Tartarus denser still, to add more corruption and more darkness! No, no, Jacques! Don't believe what books tell you. Believe in the natural uprightness of your own conscience and the clean impulses of your own manhood. Light is never refused to him who seeks it with a sincere heart. True wisdom waits outside your door. Happy are the souls who welcome her within their houses as an honored mother.

One sentence in your letter made me laugh. It was when you told me you feared that in religion you might find an end to your quest—an end to strife. Dear friend, the day you receive God, you will have a guest within you who will never leave you repose. "I have not come to bring peace, but a sword." On that day you will know the ferment no earthly vessel can contain, the true strife against passion and spiritual darkness, the real battle—not that in which a man falls, but that from which he emerges victor.

Come, then, dear boy, be brave! Be one of us, be a brother in arms, for me, as well as for that splendid fellow F——. Let us eat together, all three, the Passover which Christ desired with a great desire, the banquet which He makes for us of His own Flesh and Blood. Far from you, almost as far as the stars, and yet near your heart, a man is living whom your letter filled with joy. I read it sitting near the cradle of my own new-born child, with what confusion, with what bitter self-reproach, with what terror almost, at finding myself the instrument through which God had sent the summons to one of His creatures. Think what must be the joy, and what the humiliation, of the servant who lifts his hands toward the Master, too deeply convinced of his own unworthiness to dare raise his eyes, and cries aloud: *Unde hoc mihi?*

In all affection,

Paul Claudel

I give you a *rendez-vous?* At Pentecost—at the Table of Our Lord. And of course the confessional, first. Poor boy! I know it is hard.

But, after all, no harder for you than for others. Think of those of us who have gone before you. No human respect from you—Jacques Rivière!

To Paul Claudel

BORDEAUX, 5TH APRIL, 1907

I got your letter yesterday and have been in turmoil ever since. My misery is choking me, at last I see how low I have fallen, and the sight revolts me. Yet, at the very moment that the desire is mastering me to cry to you: "You are too cruel! Leave me alone: your pitiless kindness breaks my heart!" the idea is entering my head that I *might*, after all, yet become a Christian.

And for the first time! Hitherto I had not entertained it a moment. Even with you I had played a game—had been, if such a thing is possible, an unconscious hypocrite. How full I was of tricks and devices. I must have had a secret fear that, if I showed myself too far removed from you, too "different," you might not answer me at all. So that, even in that last letter (which contains so many things I would rather not have written), all the while I was telling you frankly of what prevented me from believing, I had the air of hinting that my belief was not invincible—that I was waiting for some refutation, that I was quite ready to welcome your advice. And all this was false—a mere parade. I wanted your reply, your exhortation to believe, I burned with curiosity to know what you would say and how you would say it. But I wanted nothing else. Yes, even when I believed myself sincere I was playing a game.

And now, how thoroughly I am punished! By what miracle does it come about that, writing to the man I represented myself to be, you find just the right words to say to the man I am? And how cruelly you overwhelm me! I no longer know whither to reach my arms; I am become so much confusion and chaos; I cannot even weep. There is something within me that writhes intolerably, that tortures me and drives me near delirium. My indifference will not return: you have stirred it too deeply: I seek blindly, knowing that my eyes are sealed. I want to weep and cannot. Try—try to understand something for which there are no words. Imagine an obscure but unceasing turmoil, an overpowering disgust, a horror for the clearness of perception that I seemed to have before, interior collapse, desires I cannot account for—for something, I know not what. Now at last I realize what true anguish can be, what it can mean to be plunged into darkness, goaded on by one incessant question, to wrestle with something formless and unknown. And at the same time, I must own the thought of losing you, the terror of being forced to a perpetual separation. For I know that if I do not soon find what I am seeking, you will not keep me as your friend.

And yet—how convinced I am that you do not understand my hesitation! In the realm of light where you live, everything must seem so evident, so joyous, so easy. You cannot understand the trouble in which I am immured. You have all the air of taking my backings and fillings for a brief struggle against human respect. And, if I do not emerge a victor, and that soon, you will withdraw the dear hand that is my only hope in the darkness. Yes, yes—it is this way and no other. Pitiless kindness! I read it between the lines of your letter, adorable for its tenderness and yet—how terribly imperious in tone!

Oh, my other soul—think a while! If you leave me, I am lost indeed. Be patient! Do not imagine that faint-heartedness keeps me back. Would anyone through mere sloth linger in the torments I am suffering? If I do not yet say, "Yes"—if I beg for delay, it is not through any fear. You are quite wrong to believe that human respect counts much with me. No. It is because I am still in the same nameless upheaval as before, because you have stirred up my soul like so much stagnant water, and I must find some way for myself out of the chaos and back to limpidity. Be merciful!

Oh, I know that you will protest—will reply that it is not your intention to abandon me so soon. But think! I shall need a year, perhaps two years, ten years, possibly a life-time before I can throw myself at God's feet. I am not the catechumen, the man already half-converted that I have let you think. I am just a miserable and anguished soul, very far from God and perhaps destined never to reach Him. Promise me not to pass out of my sight, at least!

I promise on my part to devote all my life to reaching your side. Dear brother, I need you so sorely.

Do you know that for a long time, I even thought of coming out to find you, of leaving everything behind, and joining you in the East! Now, of course, I am too much afraid. But at least it deserves to be taken into consideration that, for the sake of the help you were to me, I was ready to grasp you with my very hands. Now, you will be too sorry for me to ever leave me.

Alas, how clearly I foresee that, for years and years, delays and difficulties must be my lot! How far am I already from the man who seemed only to need the clearing up of a few difficulties before he yielded! How I reproach myself for having let you think that I was an easy quarry! Believe me, I did it unintentionally, by an instinctive fear of not interesting you, which, now that I am grown perfectly sincere, has turned into a fear of estranging you.

Can you understand how it is that just now I said the idea of becoming a Christian entered my head for the first time this morning? It is because your letter suddenly let me feel, and, as it were, *handle*, the innumerable obstacles that separate me from God. Up to now I could never conceive of myself and religion in any relationship at all. As a pure abstraction (or when my imagination was stirred by the beauty of your work), I have occasionally believed or tried to believe myself in the dispositions for conversion. But I never imagined myself a Christian in any practical sense of the word. I never thought seriously what returning to God would imply, nor of things that your letter makes me realize. It shows me that union with Him is possible, by showing me the distance that separates me from Him. I feel now that I am definitely involved in something from which I must either emerge a victor or die. Up to now I still stood outside, acting a part to make you talk. I exaggerate perhaps, but this is not far from the truth.

You will tell me, in order to encourage me, that merely to have entered the maelstrom in which I am struggling, is something. I know it. But this does not prove to me that I can ever free myself, swim clear away, deliver myself from peril by the mere act of accepting it. I may struggle, yes, strive for years and years, and go under in the end.

7TH APRIL

One convincing proof to you of my trouble might well be the disorderly fashion in which I speak of it. I make no pretence of regulating or disciplining my soul before I present it to you. With your marvelous faculty of divination, I believe you will pierce to the truth through all my cries, appeals, refusals, contradictions, and incoherences. Already, and when you hardly know anything about me, with what consummate skill you are able to speak to me! I feel you looking at and through me with a glance far less liable to error than that which I turn inward upon myself.

For I myself am so unstable, so undependable. "I shift to and fro like two roving eyes." You think to find me—and I am no longer there! In these last two days I have changed once more. The anguish which I believed your letter had instilled definitely in me has evaporated. I have fallen back anew into my horrible indifference, my detestable inertia. I read your letter over again and am barely conscious of a qualm. No longer do I feel that reaction of self-hatred, that abomination of myself, nor the desire of which I spoke to you. Obscurity settles down upon me like some false and infamous peace. Oh, I am indeed lost! How can you not perceive it? Something in me is withered; there is a lassitude, a sheer incapacity for resistance, an inherent impotency.

All this is immensely complicated by my books—the books which you tell me, with such good reason, to mistrust, the books which I have so erred in loving. It is from reading books, even those which I told you about in my first letter, and from Barrés in particular, that I contracted my fatal predisposition to sloth. I have grown used to looking at life instead of living it, to amusing myself with the play of my emotions instead of controlling them; to separating acts from thoughts and abandoning them as much vile matter. And—here is the greatest evil of all. With Barrés, I have grown to consider that sinning by mere action is not sinning at all—that the only real sin is the sin of thought. I have never learnt how to keep my soul and my life in unison. This is why, although, Christianity apart, I have always kept a high moral standard, I have never translated it into action, nor adapted my activities to it. Basely and unworthily, I suffered myself to founder. Now I am no longer in a position to exert that power of free will which is indispensable to the Christian life. I fall back upon inertia, upon that old sluggish self-contemplation, that abandonment to the force of gravity which I am thoroughly conscious (with how great terror and with how great despair!) is the unique, the unpardonable sin, the sin which is punished by eternal fire.

As for these sudden accesses of anxiety, one of which has begun to grip me anew—of what service to me will they be if they only lead me back to a new collapse and plunge me into a new and darker night? No. My weakness is past cure. Suppose even I was so overwhelmed by the terrible beauty of Christianity that intellectual conversion took place within me. I should never be able to translate it into acts, repressing them, disciplining them, controlling them, making each one the perpetual prayer to God that it should be. They would still be something apart as before, something outside myself, that drifted with the stream. Better far not to believe than to believe and not practice.

The question of human respect does not arise at all. Just because my actions are strangers to me, I should no more blush to confess them and go to communion afterwards than not to do so. What keeps me back is a far graver obstacle—the incapacity of directing my life. You tell me that youth is formed for heroism. I believe you. And yet, how incapable of it am I! Do you remember, in *Le Jardin de Bérénice*, the letter of Seneca to the risen Lazarus? For a long time this was my creed. I reread it the other day with horror, but with a horror all the greater because I felt at the bottom of my heart that it still expressed me, with all my cowardice and weakness, to a marvel. This is what is destroying me, this strange dilettantism (much as I detest the word). I have enough strength of mind to stand out against mockery, insult, general contempt. But not enough to bridle myself, to discipline myself, to force myself to tread one road and one only.

The only road! Ay, there is the terrible phrase, there is the thing in Christianity which terrifies me and against which my whole being rises up in revolt! Yes, yes—I can well believe that this admirable doctrine, which has made me shed tears of love as I read your plays, is true. But why *the* truth, the only truth? Why this single one, and no other? Why not numberless truths, to which, turn by turn, we can give our love? Why must I deny my soul to so many alien beauties just because they are alien? Knowing how much books have influenced me, you will say: This is Gide! But books only corrupt those who are predisposed by nature to receive their poison. Ever since my childhood I have been possessed, and in an extraordinary degree, by something which I have since then, christened pedantically enough, a "sentiment of the multiplicity of co-possibles." Every time I have given my adhesion to some belief, I have been keenly sensible of the existence of a host of others which deserved it quite as much. My difficulty has always been to keep my love in one channel, to forget the others—the infinite immensity of those others. And thus it comes about that every time I have been on the point of professing faith in one, of forcing my soul, so to speak, to converge upon some one point, a scruple against neglecting so many others, of seeming to undervalue so many fresh manifestations of God, has held me back. Why, I ask myself, should God be here—and not there? Dare we limit Him—conceive of Him as finite, believe that He has refused to extend His existence to infinity? To me every religion appears some one medium that God has found specially apt to speak through to some one race. That Christianity may be the most beautiful, I do not deny. That it is the only one, I cannot admit.

In tranquil fashion, you ask me something that is really terrible. You say to me: "There are many things which appear to you infinitely sweet—terribly desirable, which you will have to renounce." Yes. And it is just this which throws me into consternation. Is it true—is it true? I ask myself. Must I no longer cherish, no longer even know pleasures that smile upon me now as if challenging me to tear their loved visages from my heart? How many old friends am I to turn my back upon? Can God be so pitiless, so unjust? Think! I am a man who cannot look on beauty without a catch in his throat, for whom the mere verification of the exterior world means an invasion of delight overwhelming in its plenitude. Yet you would condemn me to a retrenchment which seems to me rather death than the initiation to new life.

You must forgive me if I seem to speak extravagantly, or if I have the air of relishing my impiety and of brazening it out to you. Down in my heart I have so strong a desire for certainty, so violent an aspiration after sincerity! All I am telling you (you will be quick to perceive it) is only a repetition, a little different in form, more open and more emphatic, of my last confession. Once again I am displaying baseness, once more I spread out my petty complexes for your benefit. But it is not to glorify them: it is to implore anew a remedy and an anodyne. I believe with all my heart that you can cure me. I beg you, I implore you, not to leave me in my abjection, but to seize my hand, to insult me—to strike me if necessary, but at least to pry me loose from my indifference and guide me to something better and higher.

Oh, my brother, I am so sick of all this meanness of soul, so disgusted with all this turmoil, all this puerile argument, when I know I should be doing better to throw myself on my knees and lay my head in the dust! What would I not give to be able to utter one cry—one cry in which my whole being should be concentrated, so loud, so pure, so resonant that I would feel regenerated merely for having uttered it: the cry of little Tintagiles, suddenly roused to his danger, which freed him from the powers of evil? Or for the exultation of Cebès, when he has won at last to peace, and feels his whole being dissolve in joy? Pray that my prayer may be heard in spite of me, that all my structure of doubt may melt away, that I may stand at last, naked before God! Help me, for I am in darkness and in great straits. Help me, brother dear!

Don't think I have made no effort. I went to Mass this very morning. I tried to pull myself together and to pray. I could remember only the Our Father. I repeated it over and over. But I could attain neither attention nor fervor. I had the same distractions from which I suffered so much when I was beginning to lose my faith. I could not imagine God as present. There were too many things to which I had to close my eyes. Why does the priest make a recitation of the Mass instead of consummating the sacrifice? This one went so fast he literally gabbled.... But I love the Gospel. There is something in it so moving, so pure and, as it were, eternal. Today we had the pilgrims of Emmaus; my heart was full as I read the sentence: "*Mane nobiscum, quoniam advesperascit et inclinata est jam dies.*"[†]

I also found a prayer of St. Augustine, which seems marvelously adapted to my own distress of mind. "You have made us for

† "Stay with us. Evening is drawing on and the day is near spent."

Yourself, oh, my God, and our heart will always be in trouble and unrest until it reposes in You." I am going to read the Gospels once again through and through. I would like to know the Bible as well, but don't know where to find it. There is so much I want you to tell me about all these things! Talk to me about the Testaments, Old and New. Tell me what are the best editions in which to read them. Help me to understand the Mass, giving me a brief commentary on the meaning of each of its phases. I have no scruple in asking you to do all these things. Are you not he "in whom I have placed my trust"? I know, too, how much good your theological explanations would do me. If I can, I will read St. Thomas. I hear, from M. F—— that you recommend him to souls who are seeking their way. But the Gospels are the great thing, are they not?

My dear big brother, what need I have of you at every instant, for help and guidance! Don't, I implore you, be discouraged with me. Write me long letters, talk to me about yourself and your life, and wherein you find strength. After having made you, for a year and a half, the sole object of my meditations, I want to feel myself nearer you. If I said anything to offend you in my last letter—I mean about priests, the forgetfulness of Christianity—you must overlook it. They were just so many little things that I had no business to say. There is no call for you even to refute them.

Nor need you demonstrate to me that you are one with the Church in your understanding of dogma. From your *Abrégé* I understand already the admirable orthodoxy of all your interpretations. Even from your plays I had already sensed all that you say in this book, though I did not then see so clearly its concordance with Christian doctrine.

There is really only one thing I implore of you. That is to save me from all this nothingness, to shake me out of my quiescence, to set my activity going, to sting me to effort. Long as the letters are I have written you, they are merely a repetition of two themes: my weakness, my inertia, both arising from my dalliance with nothingness. Cure me of this evil and—I am a believer. On my side, I promise to make desperate efforts to tear this baseness from my heart and to "escape from the sepulchre which men build for themselves."

This very day I was dreaming on the ineffable peace that might be mine if I could make up my mind to go to communion, to partake, as you bid me, of the Celestial Banquet with you, and live in God. Yes, I feel it: I am made for joy and I swear to possess it. If only you will not leave me! If only you will be my support at every hour of the day!

Thank you, my brother, for the affection with which your letter ended. Do not let me go—suffocate me rather than that!

Ever yours,

Jacques Rivière

P. S. Perhaps I shall try to go to communion on Whit Sunday. I am only waiting to be released from my military service (in a fortnight) to enter a little into myself and to examine my conscience. "Taking my bearings from where I stand." Yes. I know something about that, and will do my best.

In your next letter speak to me a good deal about divine worship and tell me what I ought to read. Tell me something also about your work, which seems to me the finest of the fine. Merely to read about it does me good.

By the way, here are a few details upon my worldly position which you ought to have. From childhood I was intended by my father for advanced studies, especially in Greek. I studied at the École Normale Supérieure, for entrance to the School at Athens. After working for two years in Paris I failed in my examinations. Against my father's will, I then determined to study philosophy and obtained my degree last year at the Bordeaux Faculty. Now, after a year in the army, I am at a loss what to do. I detest the University. I *think*, none the less, that I am under contract to it for ten years, and I shall need a certain sum of money to buy my discharge. If I go on studying at Bordeaux, I shall have a scholarship of 1,200 francs for two years. But I want to leave Bordeaux and live by myself in Paris. In that case I shall find myself without resources. What ought I to do?

I had a dream (I told you this before) of setting out for China—of leaving all my old life behind, of taking nothing with me but a changed heart. But what would I find to do out there? I suppose you do not know of any way by which I could earn a living. There can't be much that a young European without trade or profession can do at Tien-Tsin? No, I am afraid it is too fine a dream. And then, I am a little afraid of you.

* * * * *

I owe you this confession in order to merit your advice on the decision I ought to make. Tell me then, whether I should come out to you, or remain, a solitary, in Paris.

One thing more: My family, on both sides, have always been Christians. I am the first to avow myself a skeptic. Indeed, I have not dared to admit as much to my relations on the maternal side.

Such a thing would wring their hearts. And their kindness to me knows no bounds.

To Jacques Rivière
TIEN-TSIN, 25TH MAY, 1907

Innuit immensâ admiratione quod est, mira haec externis ostendendo quae non est. (St. Gregory)

My dear friend,

I had hardly put my letter in the mail when I received yours to me dated the 7th of April. Ours is a correspondence indeed! Don't think that I am reproaching you. On the contrary, it is for me the most urgent and the most pleasant of duties to try and do a little good to the young people who are going through the same crisis I went through years ago.

Just a little piece of philosophy in reply to your theory of several possible truths. In a certain sense nothing exists but God. That is to say, He alone exists by His own volition. All other creatures exist only as an act of His will (St. Paul). Since there is only one God, there can only be one Truth; the terms are synonymous. Since there is only one God there can also be only one essential fashion of differing from God, all created things having this *in common*, that they are not God. God, then, is the beginning and the end of every creature, which could only be created for His sole glory, and since there is only one truth, there can be only one certitude handed down to us by revelation. Where God is not, there can be no truth: where there is no being, there is nothing. But God is everywhere. He creates, sustains and contains all. We are the assistants at a continuous creation.

But let us leave philosophy, and enter together upon a surer road, whither I am glad to find that you yourself invite me. I mean the way of practical living. A man who wants to know the effect of brandy will find out more by drinking three glasses than by reading all the physiological handbooks on the subject in existence.

Books to read. Pascal above all. He is the veritable apostle *ad exteros* for us Frenchmen. Several books of mysticism: Angela of Foligno, Ruysbroeck, St. Teresa, the Lives of the Saints, however badly written they may be. The admirable revelations of Anne Catherine Emmerich on the life of Our Saviour. I had recommended F—— to read Bossuet's *Élevations sur les Mystères* and the Meditations upon the Gospels. Personally I admire them tremendously. But the Christianity of the seventeenth century is terribly arid and austere. Read Dante. And as much as you can find of Newman.

Practices. The Liturgy and attendance at the offices of the Church will teach you more than books. Take a plunge into that immense reservoir of glory, of certitude and of poetry. Don't expect any sudden illumination. Your darkness will disperse little by little. And whatever you are moved to do, I repeat, begin now. *Facienti quod est in se non negatur gratia.*[†] Say your prayers every day—even if only in a mechanical fashion—even if your attention is elsewhere. The will at least will be there. And who shall say that these prayers, so many times repeated by saintly lips, have not by this time acquired a virtue all their own—*ex opere operato.* Anyone who prays night and morning, with as much recollection as he can muster up (often not a great deal), is *certain* of salvation. If possible, go to daily Mass. Follow, for

† Grace is never denied to him who does his best.

one year at least, the cycle of worship of the Church. Wear a scapular, recite your rosary, make the Way of the Cross. As soon as you can manage it, try to concentrate your thoughts for at least a quarter of an hour a day upon some sentence or some story in the Gospel. When you fall, don't lose courage. Have an imperturbable faith in God's love. Remember that it is not the sins of which we are most ashamed that do us the most harm. The only thing God really hates is pride. *Cor contritum et humiliatum non despicies.*

As soon as you are converted, obey your confessor implicity. He will, doubtless, tell you to go to communion as often as possible. Practice works of active charity. (Read upon this subject the verses from the prophet Joel in the Mass for Ash Wednesday). There is no more marvelous cordial for the soul than charity. As soon as possible, become a brother of the Society of St. Vincent de Paul, to which I have had the happiness to belong for twenty years.

The Bible. It is essential that you should read this from end to end. The only edition with which I am familiar is that of Fillion. It is not a faultless one, but at least it is orthodox. However trite and irritating the commentary may be, at least it permits a primary understanding of the text, which would be difficult to tackle without it. Unhappily this edition is in six thick volumes. But someone can lend them to you.

Mass. How speak worthily of this adorable mystery? I have tried several times, and found it always beyond my competence. Assist at it, and, little by little, you will understand it. *L'Année Liturgique* of Guéranger, which I would not recommend to you otherwise, contains all the prayers at Mass, complete and in Latin.

St. Thomas. Read him when you can, but not all at once. He is an affair of years.

Poor child! Here you are—entangled in the meshes of Christ. *Induxisti nos in laqueum*: Thou has led us into a snare. I can understand your terror at the sight of this new world. For there is no use in pretending otherwise. To give up the freedom of thinking as one pleases is a great sacrifice, and no one can foretell where the demands of God, which the Scriptures tell us are harsher than Hell, will stop. Small wonder that your flesh shudders where so many of the greatest saints have trembled before you. "Every conversion is a sentence," Pascal tells us. But do not be dismayed. God knows how much you can do, and joy always outweighs the sacrifice! You will never die, death no longer means anything to you; God is yours for all eternity and will transform you into Himself that you may enjoy Him (the Deific Vision).

Some practical advice. Stay where you are and don't leave the way marked out for you. Accept the cross God gives you to carry. You can do a great deal of good at the University, and your position there will leave you a great choice of work and the liberty for reflection of which you have so much need. If God did not want you where you are, He would never have placed you there. Once in my own life, I sought to leave the beaten track for something which I thought better, and a positive catastrophe for me was the result. Perhaps Paris is the best place for you. In any case, the last thing I should advise you would be to leave France. This foreign concession life, without any sort of moral support, is death for most men, and a weakening of fibre for all. I know it only too well.

Good bye, dear friend. I see Our Lady near you, who is looking at you in silence, but with an infinite love. One day you will know it—this silence wherein God or His Mother speaks to us.

I find among my notes a few little quotations which I send you.†

Write me as often as you can. It will always give me pleasure to answer your letters.

P. Claudel

† Editor's Note: See Appendix at the end of the book.

To Jacques Rivière

TIEN-TSIN, 23RD MAY, 1907

My dear friend,

Your second letter, dated the 10th to the 23rd March, only reached me yesterday. It had been sent by way of Siberia, and had been forgotten in one of the forty-six sacks of mail which the camels of the Gobi desert had refused to bring us till just now.

I read this letter with the same interest and the same emotion as the former one. It took me back to the days of my own spiritual combat—that great ferment of "the twenties," upon which the wine of our whole life depends.

The confidence that you show in me touches me, but it also alarms me a little. You challenge me to find the word for you that cures and raises from the dead. But this word, only God and His ministers possess. I can do no more than give you a few little brotherly counsels. Let me take up the points of your letter, one by one.

Nothingness. He who denies The Being denies all being. Take the Word from the phrase and all meaning is lost. He who denies unity, denies the number made up of it. He who believes no longer in God has ceased to believe in anything. From Luther to Nietzsche, through Kant, one may trace, in perfect sequence, the degradation of man to that utter paganism of which the Hindu theories are the best expression. Take away the end of the world (which is also a beginning) and all order is at an end. What remains is simply chaos, with all its despair and horror, to which old Tathagata preferred non-being.

Thanks be to God you are not in the same darkness. The Christian revelation has dissipated it once and for all. Don't take for an incurable disease what is a passing and salutary crisis, and the index, on the contrary, of an intact and healthy soul.

What can I say to you to deliver you from this obsession with nothingness, which I have known in my own time? Nothingness—non-being, is that which does not exist. How then can that which does not exist have any existence? But I know that pure philosophic discussion is not what you want. There is no proposition to which the will to contradict cannot oppose a negative. On the other hand, the testimony of your own senses is a witness, and a powerful one, that all things pass, that they are only known to you insofar as they are passing on, in movement; in other words, insofar as they fail to exist in themselves (or as the schoolmen term it "subsist"). God alone subsists. All His creatures have their part in the nothingness from which His creation drew them, and wherein pride would plunge them anew, for it is the only thing they do not derive from Him.

To one sensible testimony I answer with another. Despite their precarious existence, all things wear the image of the eternity which contains them (in the sense of cohering) and which permits us to understand them. Matter passes on. But form persists eternally renewed, like God Himself, of which it is a partial image. The antinomy of the eleatic philosophers, revamped by Kant, comes from the fact that they represented the Infinite under the form of a straight line, an endless series of units to which another unit could always be added. But straightness is itself a rupture and a disjunction. The true image of infinity is the circle, the *zero* (in Phoenician: *seed* or egg). And, at the same time, the circle is the perfect image of the finite, of creation realized. Every living creature is a circle, more or less modified, but always limited by a contour. *Form* is the perfect, infrangible closure, having neither beginning nor end, image of that eternity, that Eternal Being, from whom not all the disciplines of Buddha and the devil put together will ever let us escape.

A second principle of solidity on which I would have you reflect is that of *homogeneity.* During the past two centuries science has pushed the frontiers of the visible world to a prodigious distance. (In this connection F——has doubtless informed you that, for reasons which I will tell you some other time, if you want to hear them, I believe neither in the infinity of the visible world nor in a plurality of inhabited worlds.) Most of the stars are placed at distances from us so enormous that these can only be calculated. Nevertheless the analytical eye of the spectroscope has been brought to bear on them and has not discovered in their composition any elements other than those of which our own planet is composed. Happily then, every issue is closed! From end to end the universe is composed of like elements, governed by, controlled by what science calls the same laws, but which I term the same *forms.* All the possible is already occupied. You yourself know the distinction between *potentiality* and *the act.* Here, before your eyes, is All-potentiality in action.

You see then, that things are not a chaos, but that, in their essence, there is order, meaning and necessity. The infinite does not preclude personality, which is form in its extremest and most rigorous aspect. Give to the sides of a rectangular triangle whatever dimensions you please, the properties of the triangle will not change.

It follows then that we are not astray—that we have certain bearings, certain reliable means of finding our way about in a region whose confusion is only apparent. If the movement of a tiny iron needle suffices to point us toward the North, and the tension of a hair to measure the humidity of the atmosphere, why should not that superior mechanism which is man give us indices as legitimate and as infallible? Why, by reason of that principle of homogeneity which I spoke of just now, should we not be able to rely on interior directives as confidently as upon a fragment of magnetised iron or a spoonful of mercury?

The supreme human fact is the desire for happiness and joy, which is not realized in this life. It has all the character, deep and crude, profound and self-evident, of a necessity, and we have no more reason to mistrust it than to mistrust our appetite when it tells us we must eat. The fact that I am not hungry just now, or that the food before me is not appetising, does not enter into the question.

From this principle the whole of Christianity derives. Paganism perceives no way of communication between God and man, and, naturally, despairs. But Christendom has a contract with God, sealed with the blood of Jesus Christ. It has positive rights, something to believe in and something to rely on.

There is nothing that so lives as the Being. There is nothing stronger than the appeal of the perfect to the imperfect which we call Love.

Complacency toward non-existence. As a matter of fact, it is not in nothingness that you take pleasure at all, since there is no such thing, but in the consciousness of your liberty, your danger and even your weakness. Very much in the same way a child, when it has been scolded, takes a bitter pleasure in being unhappy and solitary. "This at least is my own." There is a text of St. Augustine which corresponds very well to such a state of mind. "*Et ego per avaritiam meam non amittere te volui; sed volui tecum possidere mendacium, sicut nemo vult ita falsum dicere, ut nesciat ipse quid verum sit.*"† Where better than in religion do you find so profound a conviction of the nothingness of man, and, at the same time, of his dignity and his suffering? Read the terible nocturnes in the Office for the Dead. All things die. But they die in God, like a child who renders his last breath upon the bosom of a loved father, and enfolded within his arms. To die thus is a joy.

Take heart! All these little discomforts, all these symptoms which, in themselves, are an excellent thing, will disappear with the specific cure, baptism by the Spirit of Fire.

Decadence inside the Church. Of no consequence. Truth has no relation to the number of people whom it persuades. Few go to Mass today: few also understand Pindar or Parsifal. You have to answer for your own soul, not those of others. Besides, it has all been foretold: "Think you, when the Son of Man comes, He will find faith upon the earth?"

"*Are you orthodox?*" "There is but one commandment. Thou shalt love the Lord with all thy heart and with all thy strength. And the second is like unto the first. Thou shalt love thy neighbor as thyself." If there is anything else in my miserable books, I hereby renounce it, I hereby disavow it with execration. Love of God, total submission to the Church: I have never taught aught else. Read Saint John, read Saint Paul. In them you will find the truth in full splendor and glory, and will no longer need the rigmaroles of poor Claudel. How happy you will make me when that day comes!

---

† In my greed I was unwilling to let you go, but wanted to possess both You and my lie together, since no man is so in love with lying as not to recognize truth.

"I don't like priests." I did not like them either. Never have I gone through such agony as on the day of my first confession. Such a sentiment is one more inspiration of the Evil One. It is (be it said *cum grano salis*) the horror those possessed by him feel for Jesus Christ. Persevere, in spite of it. You will soon get over such unworthy prejudices.

I know that you are suffering. But this suffering is only honorable on condition that you emerge from it a victor. Otherwise it is nothing finer than that "puppy distemper" of which Barrés speaks. One of two things: either you will become a Christian, or the tasks and pleasures of life will cure you quickly of all your metaphysical worries. Many people write to me, but few have courage enough to put their salvation before their pride. They are like the young man in the Gospels, who asked so earnestly to be told the way to the Kingdom of God, and "went away sadly" when it was shown him. Don't let me believe that you are one of these poor creatures: rather that I may really call you my brother.

I have answered you as best I can. Do not expect from me an exact reply to all your misgivings. There will always remain a part of your warfare that you must wage alone, there will always be thorns that only perseverance wears down. But grace is never denied the man who does his best. *Facienti quod est in se non negatur gratia.* I can go on weaving my philosophies. But truth is something far simpler, something as natural as sunshine or spring water, as palatable spiritually as bread and wine. And do not believe that acceptance of Christianity means dulled wits or a mutilitated intelligence. There are people who believe that absinthe and the café-concert are indispensable items of existence and are surprised at anyone who gets on without them. An illuminated mind—a heart delightfully cleansed, and a rightly-ordered will—these are the effects of Christian discipline. The Christian is one who knows what he is doing and where he is going in the midst of beings who are far worse than brutes, and who no longer know the difference between good and evil, yes and no. Amid a generation of cripples and alcoholics, he stands out like a god, not through any merit of his own, but simply because he has put himself in harmony with the natural order by submitting where submission is due. He is a free man among slaves.

Affectionately,

Paul Claudel

To Jacques Rivière
27TH MAY, 1907

On the Mass.

"It is not the invocation merely, but, if I dare use the word, the evocation of the Eternal. He becomes present on the altar in flesh and blood, before whom angels bow and devils tremble. This is that awful event which is the scope, and is the interpretation, of every part of the solemnity. Words are necessary, but as means, not as ends; they are not mere addresses to the throne of grace, they are instruments of what is far higher, of consecration, of sacrifice. They hurry on as if impatient to fulfil their mission. Quickly they go, the whole is quick; for they are all parts of one integral action. Quickly they go, for they are the awful words of sacrifice; they are a work too great to delay upon; as when it was said in the beginning: 'What thou doest, do quickly.' Quickly they pass, for the Lord Jesus Christ goes with them, as He passed along the lake in the days of His flesh, quickly calling first one and then another. Quickly they pass; because, as the lightning which shineth from one part of Heaven unto the other, so is the coming of the Son of Man. Quickly they pass, for they are as the words of Moses, when the Lord came down in the cloud, calling on the Name of the Lord as he passed by. 'The Lord, the Lord God, merciful and gracious, long suffering and abundant in goodness and truth.' And as Moses on the mountain, so we too 'make haste and bow our heads to the earth and adore.' So we, all around, each in his place, with his own heart, with his own wants, with his own thoughts, with his own intention, with his own prayers, separate but concordant, watching what is going on, watching its progress, uniting in its consummation—not painfully and hopelessly, following a hard form of prayer from beginning to end, but like a concert of musical instruments, each different, but concurring in a sweet harmony, we take our part with God's priest, supporting him, yet guided by him. There are little children there, and old men and simple labourers, and students in seminaries, priests preparing for mass, priests making their thanksgiving: there are innocent maidens, and there are penitent sinners: but out of these many minds rises one enthusiastic hymn, and the great action is the measure and scope of it. And you ask me…whether this is not a formal, unreasonable service! … *O Sapientia, fortiter suaviterque disponens omnia! O Adonai, O Clavis David et expectatio gentium, veni ad salvandum nos, Domine Deus noster!*" (Newman, *Loss and Gain*)

To Paul Claudel

BORDEAUX, 4TH JULY, 1907

Your last letter threw me into the same profound confusion of spirit as your first. I was waiting for it before beginning a definite examination of conscience. There were certain things I wanted stated in precise terms. I wanted to have a clear mind and an absolutely impartial judgment when I faced the terrible alternatives. For a moment these statements, which I desired so keenly, carried me off my feet, and it was only by a great effort that I recovered my balance. Now I have looked, in cold blood, upon what God, according to you, would exact of me. I have examined myself with the most meticulous care, asking myself whether submission were possible. And I realize that any sort of agreement, any measure of welcome to His demands, is not only unrealizable today, but unimaginable in the future.

Before you blame me, try at least to imagine the courage it takes me at a moment like this, to put the facts before you in all their brutal frankness. Never, never will you know the distress that it costs me to own myself thus irreparably separated from you. It is ten days ago now since your letter reached me. I have spent the interval racked by indecision, literally not daring to make up my own mind.

And now, it is all over. I have told you everything. Already you despise me, esteem me an outcast, a lost man in a living world, one to be ignored henceforth. And yet, it seems to me, I owe you an explanation of the incompatibility which I have discovered between myself and God. It is you yourself who unwittingly pronounced my condemnation when you told me that "the only thing God hates is pride." *Cor contritum et humiliatum non despicies.* For a long time I had not understood myself. I was not aware that I was, beyond anything else, inherently and profoundly a proud man. One day I was explaining to M. F——, very much as I am explaining to you now, what kept me from believing: my consciousness of eternal nothingness, my complaisance in that miserable knowledge and so on. "Why," he exclaimed, "this is pride!"

I felt at once that he was right. Until then, I suppose, I had lived in such intimacy, in such fusion, with my pride, that I had never perceived it. Very much as other men fail to perceive their humility. But that day I looked into my heart and saw what I *really was*—pride, pride, *pride*! My thoughts, my words, my very gestures—nothing but pride. You tell me that I am already saved, because I see myself so clearly, have probed my evil so accurately. No, and again, no! For I refuse, my whole being refuses, to call such a thing an evil. How could I? To do so would be to deny myself. Since all my being is pride, since whatever there is of me is pride and nothing else, would I not be denying myself? As a matter of fact, my whole life is spent in an intense rapture with myself, in other words with the pride which seems to you such a disease. I am never done secretly flattering myself for being the man I am. I am not even like the immoralist who says: "My God, I praise Thee for making me so admirable a creature." No, but: "I praise *myself* for having made *myself* a creature so admirable." Do not make the mistake of confounding the inhibitions of this pride with mere human respect, with that petty and almost physical repulsion some men have to bow the head. Last Sunday I prostrated myself before the Blessed Sacrament without the slightest hesitation. But, though I can bend the knee, I cannot bow my soul. With a madness and rashness which you will consider impious, I desire it shall be upright and inflexible, no matter what storms may assail it. Yes, *Tête d'Or*, if you will. But even his death does not dismay me. At least he *lived*.

Was I, then, guilty of hideous hypocrisy in appealing to you, in complaining of soul-sickness, in begging you for a remedy? No! But what cried out to you was a transitory feeling: a momentary dissatisfaction, wounded pride, and desire for support. It is such a lonely thing to be proud! Besides, I had grown to love you; so great an enthusiast was I where you were concerned, that it seemed to me anything you said would only exalt me still more. All this I felt confusedly, in a sort of vague anguish that I took for a real desire for spiritual peace.

Of course, it was no such thing. For, listen (oh, will you ever forgive me for this?)—I do not want joy, I reject joy, I do not want immortality! You tell me I shall die no more if I am one with God. But I want to die! I want only myself. Life, even though it should be one long ordeal, is enough for me so long as it is *my* life. I had much rather suffer than consent to domination, yes, though it lasted but a moment and secured me an eternity of beatitude.

You will think, perhaps, that these are blasphemies, suggested to me by the Evil One. No. I write them in cold blood, without a tremor, with no sensation save one of unhappiness at destroying the friendship which was already inclining you towards me. Try to understand how it was possible for me, even after my own deceptions were at an end, to deceive you anew, to make you accept my shifts and evasions with a whole host of plausible motives. I love you too dearly not to prefer losing you to going on abusing your friendship in this indefinite fashion. This is why I have gathered all my forces together to send you a letter that it is torture for me to write. I only ask you to try to think the better of me for it.

You see how I cannot turn one inch without finding the thorn of pride against my soul. Yes—at this very moment I am proud of my courage and brutality, and being ashamed of being proud of it does not lessen the pride a bit.

What roots this pride has sent down in me! From childhood I have been perfecting and refining it. I used to create little humiliations for myself in order to have the pride of not having feared them. If you knew by what subtleties I surrounded my state of grace at the time of my first communion! I purified my purity, I invented little scruples, in which I gloried, then humbled myself for having gloried, then glorified myself for having humbled myself for glorying. And so on—*ad infinitum*. And already I felt this to be so sweet, that, with a resolution that astounds me as I remember it, I renounced all other happiness, all promise of other joys, in advance. From childhood I rejected happiness, saying, secretly: "I shall always have *myself*, there will always be *me*." And truly, I have always had this *me*, have never had enough of this *me*. I wanted it precious, glorious, fragile, this *me*: I decorated it with inconceivable refinements. At certain moments I felt that there was nothing I would not sacrifice to pride, and to the beauty of my *me*. Even its insufficiencies gave me pleasure. Were they not so many stimulants to still further perfecting it?

How lamentable all this must seem to you! With your robust certitude, you live altogether in God, you are in fusion, in perpetual communion with Him. I must have the air (for all my horror of the cheap and obvious) of playing the vulgar part of the satanist.

Beside you I must appear a creature full of malice. You do well to despise me.

Above all, to think that it is in this spirit I welcome your words of counsel and comfort, your advice gentle as though to a sick friend! I must seem to you like a malingerer who, after begging to be nursed and coddled, suddenly flings off the coverlets and jumps out of bed.

Such, however, I am. And I shall not change! I could only change by preferring someone else to myself and by becoming an object of disgust to myself. And I love myself, I love myself so intensely! This is the very expression I once used as a child, one time I happened to be alone, and seizing my wrist in my hand. I "love myself" at all times, not only for what might pass as good points, but for my miseries, my shames, my secret turpitudes and every malady of my soul. Such am I and such I shall remain. As I have made myself so shall I render myself to Him who conceived my being.

I am in no "trap set by Christ." What would Christ have to do with such as me, save to damn me? I am free—free, and I will die only of being alone.

I will say no more! What is the use of pushing to ostentation an avowal that I wanted of the coldest and most precise sincerity? Especially as I feel that I have already destroyed any affection you had for me.

And yet—oh, you whom I have called my brother, is it true that we are destined to be separated for ever? How came it that when I read you I had such a keen desire for your moral support, that I felt myself so *called* to you? I don't believe there was anything supernatural in my impulse. But truly there was something strange in my idea of writing to you. Even now, I long to know that I am not lost forever to you, that you will remember me sometimes.

Perhaps in spite of myself and through the sheer necessity of being sincere, I have made the shadows in what I wrote you just now too black. I remain persuaded of God's existence. I accept myself as I am, ineffable and unknowable. Only I refuse to prefer God to myself. I persist in believing that He asks from us nothing save the perfect and integral development of ourselves. Now you see that I am not impious. So perhaps we can still speak to one another without hatred—even understand one another from time to time. Don't give me up altogether! Keep your promise to answer my letters—to instruct and sustain me.

I am going to read the books you recommend me. I am sure I shall find great profit in them. How long I have waited to know the Bible!

And how grateful I am to you for sending me your two new books! *L'Art Poétique*, of which I had already read about three-quarters (M. F.——lent me your *Traité sur Connaissance*) is admirable. It makes so many things clear.

I may write a study on *Paul Claudel: Christian Poet* for *l'Occident.* Don't be afraid. There will be none of my little objections in it. I think the many readers who already admire you as our greatest poet should be shown that all your work has, first and foremost, a religious significance, and that its aim is instruction. If only to disturb their complacency—theirs too...!

Of course if such an article would be the least bit disagreeable to you, it goes without saying that it will never be printed. If you say nothing upon the subject in your next letter (you see, in spite of all, I expect an answer) I shall consider that I may go ahead with the article.

L'Occident is probably going to publish a little "Divagation" of mine. If you read it, please don't take it too seriously. It is vague and might easily be misunderstood. It was my pride again, which often plays me such mean tricks, that drove me to write it. I am sorry already!

I must stop here. Not being very well able to add anything to the many cruel things I have written, I close by begging you one last time more not to give me up!

Jacques Rivière

To Paul Claudel

FRIDAY, 5TH JULY, 1907

My letter, dated yesterday, the 4th of July, is in answer to yours of the 25th of May, received by me on June 24th. The letter I am writing answers yours of the 23rd of May, which I received only this morning. Our correspondence has got twisted.

It follows that when I wrote those terrible things yesterday, *I had not seen* this passage, which absolutely overwhelms me now as I read it:

> Either you will become a Christian or the tasks and pleasures of life will cure you quickly enough of all your metaphysical worries. Many people write to me. But few have courage enough *to put their salvation before their pride....* Don't let me believe that you are one of these poor creatures, rather that I may really call you my brother.

Oh, the temptation to ask you to wait for me still, to tell you that I am coming, that I am going to fight down my pride! And it would be only partly untrue. There are times when I would like to cast everything away and lose myself, with you, in God. Have you not already changed me a little, brought me nearer to Christianity, made me understand that my hatred of priests was a silly and childish attitude, given me a new taste and relish for Holy Writ?

But, no! I must shake off this desire to be a hypocrite. I cannot, I *cannot* be a Christian.

I cannot: and the best proof is that, if I could, I would be one already. You answer my objections admirably, you drown them in a positive flood of truth. I agree, I understand, I renounce all I have said. But (oh, that terrible word "but," and how necessary to utter it!), something persists, some objection hardly to be put into words—original malice, if you will—but in which I believe very deeply, and which I cannot tear out of my heart.

Everything that makes it impossible for me to believe—my contentment with nothingness, inertia, irony, pride—just as I have enumerated them for your benefit, are so many variations of this primordial refusal, which comes from my soul and which is stronger than I—oh, stronger far than I!

What can I add? Why should I go on hoping against hope for a cure? If I have not been cured in the crisis through which I have just passed, the reason must be that I am incurable. All the more incurable because I can find myself wondering whether I am really sick. No! Neither the pleasures nor the tasks of life will ever cure my metaphysical worries. These have already gone. Or, rather, they have taken the shape of a despair, profound, silent, all-inclusive and not to be shaken. I am resigned to universal vanity. Even the *grotesqueries* of the Romantic school have not been able to break me of this. Is there any better proof of sincerity that I could offer you?

I suppose then, that we are never to know one another, that you are never to speak to me as brother to brother, using the name which I usurped in order to implore your help! It is so hard for me to believe that such a renunciation, bitterer far than any Christianity would exact, is before me. I make it because I must, because I am as I am and will never change now. Yes—I am one of those "poor creatures" who put their pride before their salvation.

In the midst of my distress and sorrow, I beg you for forgiveness.

J. R.

Can it be possible that I am never going to receive another letter from you?

To Jacques Rivière

TIEN-TSIN, 4TH AUGUST, 1907

My dear friend,

I am just in receipt of your two letters, of the 4th and 5th of July.

Get rid at once of any idea that you have said some terrible, irremediable thing to me—that I am going to abandon you—that all is over between us, etc. My life is spent among people to whom God means very little and books that take small account of Him, and it is not likely that, at the age of thirty-nine I am still prone to scandal or indignation. There is nothing out of the way in finding a young man of your age aghast before the inexorable truth and before all it demands in the shape of acceptance and renunciation. The first instinct of St. Paul himself was to shy (*calcitrare*), like his own horse, at the revelation. God will speak to you in His own time. It may be the first—it may be the eleventh hour. I did wrong to be less patient than He.

But what a sad affair—this life to which you resign yourself! Look at the terrible misery of the world around you, and then consider that you can never be of any help to it—you, to whom the leisure God has given you makes it a duty, for you as for every man of good will, to seek and find the truth. Your pride and that terrible bourgeois contentment of yours is not going to be of great help to the starving and the disinherited!

I understand perfectly well that you are exaggerating when you speak to me of your pride. And yet, suffer me to be sincere in turn.

Granted that both you and I have our little faults, at least let us not cherish them as our household gods, enshrine them like so many hideous little idols. No! There is never anything fine about evil. It is always stupid and cheap. *Mali nulla substantia.* It is made up of disorder and misdirected choice. Pride is not a sign of strength but of weakness. The Fathers term it "spiritual lechery" and compare the proud man to the "effeminate" of whom the prophets have something to say. How much further advanced are you when you say: "I will not serve"—*non serviam*, like a broken glass or a blunt tool. You love yourself? Very well! Experience will not fail to cure you, and to enlighten you upon the subject of yourself with all the brutality needful.

You tell me, "I cannot be a Christian": like a man who repeats, "I cannot see," and refuses to open his eyes. I know perfectly well that it is not your intelligence which is in want of light, but your will which needs to be purified, strengthened and regulated. I have tried to indicate the therapeutic agents for such a cure, the most important of which is a return to the authorized physician, in other words, the priest. You take for insurmountable obstacles what are really nothing but suggestions that come from sloth, indecision and, as you put it very well yourself, from the devil. To cure yourself of a physical illness you would go to the ends of the earth. But when it is a question of the salvation of your poor soul, the least obstacle, the first difficulty you meet, discourages and crushes you. No, you are not satisfied with yourself and that, in itself, is a symptom. Why should the stomach and the conscience be built any differently? Why believe in what one tells you—one, and not the other? When you have so much pain at your heart, it is because there is something in Jacques Rivière that ought not to be there.

In both your letters there is one very serious thing that troubles me greatly: It is when you say you feel yourself *called* towards me. In that case, God must be behind your impulse. And if the call has been in vain, it must be because it did not find me, as it should have found me, fasting and praying. This is only too literally true, and you must never use such a phrase as "communion and fusion in God" lightly to me again. It fills me with positive horror to think that such words can be used in my regard, as though I were some kind of saint! I am nothing but a poor worlding, full of business and family affairs, relishing the good things of this world (and of the next)—in my own mediocre and banal fashion, leading a life that is full of sloth and self-indulgence, punctuated from time to time with a realization of my own unworthiness of the bitterest and most humiliating description. We are just poor children together; with God as our common Father, who will surely have pity on our unutterable absurdity as individuals.

Please forgive me for being of so little real help to you. Write me as often and as much as you like. I will always answer your letters. But do not write me as though I were your confessor and you some devout penitent making a story of your little difficulties. Rather be as one who seeks with all his heart the means to a cure. In all affection I grasp your hand.

Claudel

Reading your letter over again, I notice that you believe in God, but that you want a God who is discreet, not too exacting and comfortingly unknowable. "The perfect and integral development of yourself." There is no such thing as perfect and integral development, unless it is proportioned to its end, and this, for mankind, is God. Man is created neither *by* himself nor *for* himself, but by and for God.

Facienti quod est in se non negatur gratia. Conversions are always the result, not of some great pitched battle, but of a long series of little efforts carried to a successful conclusion. In other words, the machine that is functioning amiss must be made to function aright. You must mortify your subconsciousness little by little. You must create a Catholic atmosphere for yourself, live in the world (how admirable a world!) of Christian thought and beauty, *learn* your religion (probably you are completely ignorant of it), acquire the habit of speaking to God every day, were it only for a few moments, were it only to tell Him that you do not believe in Him and that He bores you; reflect every evening on what you have accomplished during the day, *above all practice alms-giving* and visit the poor; this will soften your heart. Have patience, and don't take every failure and every whim of vanity or self-love for a peremptory reason and an insuperable obstacle.

To Paul Claudel

BORDEAUX, 3RD OCTOBER, 1907

I have waited a month before attempting to answer you, and the reason is that I have been asking myself all the time whether I had anything left to say. Sometimes it seemed to me that everything had been said on my side, and that you had won the argument. I felt something very like remorse in remembering the incoherent complaints, the tumult of questions with which I had overwhelmed you. I regretted them all the more because I realized how clearly and how fully you found answers for them, without, however, satisfying or convincing me. You had made me thoroughly ashamed of "making a story of my little difficulties, like some devout penitent to her confessor," and of having forced you to explanations which I did not find decisive.

Now it seems to me that I have something better to say and a more essential question to put to you. I want to stop enumerating, in my rather absurd fashion, all the subjective reasons for my disbelief, and to ask you why one *must* be a Christian—why, in your opinion, there is a necessity for having a God, a religion, and a code of worship. Oh, I concede that the world is chaos, that disorder and upheaval surround us on every side! I admit that Catholicism gives us the *only* possible explanation of this chaos, that it *alone* gives some meaning to nature. But why must there be an explanation of any sort? Why must nature have any meaning at all? Why should there be a "primeval order" and a "violation" of this order? Here is where I cannot see necessity. What compels me to believe that there is in creation anything good or bad, high or low, beautiful or hideous? What legitimates the transition from my desire to the reality of the object of this desire? May it not be merely because I feel the need, in order to understand the world, of assuming that there is a certain order in this world? I cannot see why it is indispensable that the universe should have intention, end or meaning. On the contrary it appears to me rather "the eternal automaton in indefinite suspension," the vainest, the most gratutious of comedies, a farce played out by nothingness.

Will you allow me to say that you appear, to me, to admit a host of *a priori* reasons which seem to derive from this assumption: "In order that I may not despair, there must be some meaning in what I see. Therefore there is a meaning in what I see." "Take a word away from the phrase," you tell me, "and it loses its meaning." I retort: "Add a word to the phrase and it takes on a meaning." You also say: "The Christian is one who knows what he is doing and where he is going, in the midst of beings who are far worse than brutes, and who no longer know the difference between good and evil—yes or no." I think that no difference does exist, that it is quite indifferent whether a man kills his father or refrains from killing him. Nothing proves to me that we are better than senseless brutes. This will seem to you like blasphemy of the most terrible kind because your own Christianity has prevented your seeing with what insolence life makes a mockery of the distinction between "good or evil, yes or no."

Once again I must appear to you puerile and even absurd. Consider, nevertheless, the radical impossibility of proving the objective existence of "values." There is nothing Nietzschean in what I am saying now. I am not pretending to "subvert values"—to call good evil or *vice versa.* I simply deny all values and the principle of incontrovertibility. I find it easy to believe that a thing can be, and, at the same time, not be. My incapacity to conceive it does not signify a whit. In one word: I accept chaos. I have no desire to discern a face or features therein. I see nothing anywhere save nullity and absence of meaning.

You will retort that all this must be making me suffer, since I complain of it to you, and implore some solution. I am suffering from it at this moment, I suffer from it at times to such an extent that my whole life is poisoned. It is the very anguish of which I have told you, the very sentiment of nothingness which from time to time clutches and chokes me. But what does this prove? Does it prove that something exists outside of me which makes me feel the full atrocity of my condition, that there is some point of comparison by which I can measure the odiousness of life? Why should any idea I may have of a universal harmony signify that there *is* a universal harmony or that it is invisible to one who is not a Christian? May I not have invented this idea, in opposition, and by very contrast to the disorder I am forced to note? I repeat: Nothing authorizes me to pass from the reality of the idea to the reality of its content.

I foresee that in the very hunger we feel to understand you will go on finding an argument for understandableness. This does not seem legitimate to me. It is you who close your eyes in order not to see things as they are, who dazzle yourself with your beautiful inward dream, and who forget—as you lose the memory of the cruel light outside—that it is a dream and nothing more.

I am so young that it must seem ridiculous for me to evince such pessimism to one who has lived so much longer, and, it may well be, seen so much more sorrow. My sole excuse is that pessimism is the sincerest part of me, that it was born with me, that it is so attached to my soul by now that I never dream of parading it, that I never speak of it to anyone but you, and that in me it only appears outwardly through some sudden and involuntary expression which I check on my lips. But—and this I implore you to believe—never, never has the thought entered my head that there is a reason for what goes on, any order in the world or any happiness possible for mankind. I have always laughed instinctively at the fine philosophical interpretations, the cosmologies, so carefully contrived to show us that everything is in its place in the best of all possible worlds. When I came across your work first, I was struck by the bottomless anguish of Cébès, by the "Nothing Is" of Besme, by the terrible disquiet that runs through *Tête d'Or*. But it was only later, and when I was already possessed by you, that the luminous and triumphant quality of your argument dawned upon me. At that moment I had a positive ray of hope; I realized that you had undertaken to find an explanation of our chaos, food for our hunger, a remedy for the old malady which I had come to believe incurable. I felt too that the explanation was quite admirably adequate, that Catholicism took everything into account, and could satisfy every human need. It was at this period that I wrote you, asking confirmation of my hopes. If my transports led you to think that I was almost converted, it was because I thought so myself.

Then your admirable elucidations began to reach me. More and more, I felt how satisfactory they were. At the same time I realized that I could not accept the solutions you offered. I gave you a series of reasons that were really so many subjective obstacles and in whose authenticity I believed at the time. Now, as a certain chill takes the place of this crisis, I perceive the truth. Down in my heart I had no need of explanations at all. I was resigned, and had been for a long time, to see nothing but nothingness and chaos around me and before me—vanity, irrationality, everywhere! I did not want to understand, because there was nothing to understand, because this universe, of whose very existence I am uncertain, is the most useless—the most gratuitously vain that can be conceived. I no longer even complain of it. My mind was made up years ago. I can live in it alone. I can live in it while despising it.

Very likely you will accuse me of once more flattering myself in my sins, of once more making confession a pretext for pride. On the contrary: I have tried to be cold and literal, and not to borrow any adventitious aid from my incapacity and weakness.

Please forgive me this new letter, which really gets nowhere, and answer it, however difficult I make it for you to answer.

I have decided to go to Paris.

* * * * *

The article which I wrote you about will shortly appear, either in *L'Occident* or *La Grande Revue*, under the title of *Paul Claudel: Christian Poet.* A copy is to be sent you. I hope you will not be too displeased nor think that I misrepresent you unduly.

I have been reading the Bible, especially the Old Testament, which I knew only by *l'Histoire Sainte.* What can I say to you about it that would not be literary shop? I have also read Newman (*The Development of Christian Dogma, Meditations and Prayers*). He is a fine and moving writer. I am going to read Catherine Emmerich.

What do you think of this philosophico-religious movement that is being started by Père Laberthonnière, M. Blondel and M. Le

Roy? I have heard it called "protestant." It seems to me a man taking such a position would have to be a juggler to keep his footing without overstepping the bounds of Catholicism. I know a young abbé who is crazy about these people, and who is afraid that your assertions are over-dogmatic. I am not. I think that faith should be faith.

Pray believe that I think of you always, with a fervor, a respect and an affection, that would be hard to put into words.

Yours,

Jacques Rivière

To Jacques Rivière

TIEN-TSIN, 24TH OCTOBER, 1907
FEAST OF ST. RAPHAEL THE ARCHANGEL

My dear friend,

I was very glad to get your letter. I was afraid I had spoken a little harshly to you in my last letter without intending it, and I feared a long interruption to the conversation we have been having for some months. I also fear it is not going to end quite so soon in the fashion I had hoped. But, after all, it is not to the Jacques Rivière of today that I am writing, but to the man who will be Jacques Rivière twenty—forty years from now. Seed does not sprout in a day. There are certain phrases that I myself read and then carried about in my head ten years and more, before I perceived their real meaning. Perhaps some day, when I have been dead a long time, you will recall some word or other of mine, which was inspired by the most sincere affection for you.

All the objections which are the burden of your last letter may be resumed in the destestable phrase of that hideous writer Renan, which disgusted me even before I was a Christian. "After all, *perhaps* the truth is sad!" As I have said, I was not then a Christian. But already I understood that the choruses from Antigone and the Ninth Symphony were celestial documents. At the bottom of my heart I knew that a great and divine joy is the only reality, and that the man who does not admit it will never attain either to artistry or sanctity, but merely to the pretentious attitudes of the professional man of letters with his garlands of paper flowers. This is the tragedy of Stéphane Mallarmé, or any other pure artist, conscious that there is really nothing for him to say.

And here we reach the great conflict between the obective and subjective, which you are not the first to challenge me with. Kant is a great philosopher and a man whom I admire and honor. But he has been vastly misunderstood, and he invented a vocabulary which has befogged many and many a brain.

However, let us admit the distinction exists, and from the disorder that has grown up around it, let us detach the points which seem proven and indisputable to us both.

First of all, let us agree that no doubt can exist as to the reality of your own suffering. I am not inquiring just now whether or no it calls for a remedy, but whether or no it presupposes a cause, and I suppose you will agree with me that this cause is the fundamental disproportion which exists between the necessities of your heart and the satisfactions they find. This phenomenon is a general one. It is so uniform that I claim it as an *objective fact* to which you are merely one more witness. The human intelligence—the human heart, do not find in this world any end proportionate to their power and their scope. If anyone cares to deny this proposition let him name me the ends, remembering that each object is particular, and that the intelligence concerns itself with the general.[†] Riches, the satisfaction of our physical desires, can stupefy and stifle this need. They do not satisfy. Analysis would prove this immediately.

On the other hand, all rhetoric to the contrary notwithstanding,

---

† "Show us the Father (the generator) and we will be satisfied" (St. Philip).

we find that outside of our selves all things are very frankly and fitly adapted to *their* end, which is, to exist and to perpetuate themselves in the plenitude of their nature, and through the mutual concurrence of one with another. If we seem to perceive a state of (relative) disorder among them, and of warfare (too much importance must not be attached to these, for the first permits being to go on and the second affects only the modality or manner of being), I offer you this reason (without touching now upon any drawn from the doctrine of original sin): Each and every one, being an image of God, is animated by a tendency towards the infinite, which the presence of the others checks and restrains.

Here, then, is the situation. Outside of man, a certain order, which you cannot deny. Within man, a disorder which you cannot deny, either, since it is the basic reason of the letters you write me.

You do not, then, find yourself confronted with a completely disordered world; that is to say, a world where things proceed one after another at haphazard, but, on the contrary, with a world where they have adapted themselves to maintain a certain status, a certain cycle, always the same—the cycle of the year. If things were calculated for non-existence, they would not exist. What you find yourself faced with is a world in *partial* disorder, and disordered on one supreme and central point. Everything indicates, as clearly as though a finger were pointing it out, not the presence, but the absence of some essential.

Here, by the way, let me repudiate the distinction between the subjective and the objective. Everything, subjective and objective alike, forms part and parcel of a solid whole, homogeneous in the strictest sense of the word. I cannot see why an evident spiritual disposition should not constitute the subject of an inquiry and be quite as authentic and verifiable as the antenna of an insect. Upon a certain category of realities it brings to bear a testimony of which no other is capable. Why must what you call subjective be considered as a dream and an illusion? Why may we not attribute to it the same documentary value as to some concrete object? In advancing this plea, I do not, as you allege, beg the question at all. I do not say: I desire such and such a thing, therefore it exists.[†] But I do say: I desire such and such a thing, therefore, I have not got it, therefore I am for lack of it kept from some end which it would constitute for me, therefore I am not in harmony in relation to it, therefore, in relation to it, I am in a state of disorder. For the moment, this is the only point which I desire to establish.

Everything that exists is the result of a series of things differing in their nature, and, both by its constitution and its condition, forms an order. The name which you give it designates a certain order which has called it into existence.

On the one hand, then, outside of man, order exists on every point, since you cannot designate anything whose end either has not been attained or is capable of attainment; while, as regards man, the proper end is impossible of attainment in this world. What I call the *end* here, is simply the means, acquired outside himself, to maintain himself as an integer. I am taking it now in its concrete sense of closing or clinching. On the other hand, where man is concerned there is disorder. Created for the general and not for the particular, the condign object of his consideration is out of his possession.

What you find yourself disposed to acquiesce in, is not a general chaos, but a partial disorder. And that is something you cannot

---

† Which, by the way, would be as perfectly legitimate as hunger, in regard to food.

do. As Pascal has said, we must take sides. You are not an isolated unit in the midst of nature. Every being is obligated to fulfil his end, and, just as there is a physical obligation, so, far above it, a moral obligation exists. The error of the so-called Kantians is to distinguish several series of antagonistic realities, rather than superimposed realities which do not exclude one another. Where perception ends, duty begins, but in no case are we left without a guide. If you fail to fulfil your end, you become an atrophied organ, a nuisance to yourself and others. Your solitude and your contempt will not carry you very far. There is a point where reason halts and revelation comes to meet it. As the psalmist puts it: *Misericordia et veritas obviaverunt sibi, justitia et pax osculata sunt*—mercy has advanced to greet reason, and grace has embraced justice.

Let us, for the moment, leave a discussion that might lead us far afield. If we enter the domain of general objections, we find a vast territory open before us. You have not yet even touched upon the one which, in my eyes, is the gravest of all, namely, the problem of evil, nor upon those which are the most irritating and intricate, namely, questions of criticism and exegesis. Do what I will, I shall never be able to render Catholic truth obvious to you. God has not willed that it should be so. What He demands from us is a free and generous effort of our will. "*Vere tu es Deus absconditus*: truly Thou art a hidden God!" Do not dream that the mere fact of being a Christian solves all difficulties *ipso facto*, or that solution is no longer withheld once a man has entered the Church. Nevertheless, once you are one with us, all these disputes will seem to you more irritating than serious or vital.

The real obstacle in you (I know it) does not lie here. What I am fighting against in you is your rebellious youth, intolerant of bit or rein, of anything, indeed, that cramps its ardor for new knowledge and new sensation. And yet—! What world is better worth discovering than that of eternal truth, forever fresh, forever young? Men who have no knowledge of it always have the effect upon me of cripples or eunuchs. You will have, it is true, to deprive yourself of certain pleasures that defile your soul and lead nowhere. In exchange you will know steel and iron, the hale, martial, athletic joys of victory over yourself. You will do good, you will be one who has passed the test and has been assigned his place, you will know the ineffable joy of a good conscience, the confidence of a son who is with his Father, you will be at peace with everything that exists. Then you will no longer accuse the world of being savage and incomprehensible. You will become a partaker in the benediction that falls upon all God's innocent creation.

It was very kind indeed of you to publish that article upon me. I have read the one that appeared in *l'Occident.* You have the real stuff of a writer in you. I say this without felicitating you upon it especially. There are many callings that I prefer to that of a literary man.

I know very little of the philosophy of the persons you mention, and I have, in their regard, very little curiosity or interest. I do know that the books of two of them have been condemned by the Holy See. There are people who are ashamed of dear old Mother Church. They want to dress her out in the latest fashion, with straight-fronted corsets and cloche hats. They are more ridiculous than dangerous. They make me think of the poor people who were once so scared by the imposing apparatus of modern science, that they tried to get Genesis into line with the "discovery" of evolution or the theories of Laplace. Today the edifice of modern science is cracked to its very foundation, and where are all these trembling apologists now?

I am very glad to hear that you have taken up a course in Christian reading. Go to Notre Dame (it was there my own conversion took place), and try to pray before that lovely statue of the Virgin where I have knelt so often. Give her my love, and believe me affectionately yours,

P. Claudel

To Paul Claudel

PARIS, 7TH DECEMBER, 1907

My dear friend,

How shall I ever thank you enough for your overwhelming kindness to me? So then—neither my childish histrionics, nor my syllogisms of stupidities, nor my little irritations swollen into great despairs, have tired you out. Each time you start afresh with the same patience, determined to lead me towards joy.

I must tell you one great secret! Since my last letter I have felt a light dawning in me. Oh, it is not yet the light of Christianity, it is only a vague glow. But it is growing! Yes, it seems to me now that perhaps joy exists. I dare not say any more. I am waiting, waiting for some revelation to arrive that will show me form and substance in this radiance. I have not reached any settled state of calm or peace. There are still times when the old anguish assails me, when I find myself wrestling with nothingness and flung to the ground by it. I blaspheme worse than before, if only because my fall has been from a greater height. Then, when I seem to have no strength left even to despair, like some far beacon at night, which a tree had hid from my eyes, the far glow appears once more. Oh, I try so hard to be calm—to be cold! But, verily, if this is all real, if joy exists still, I yearn for it.

No, no, don't imagine that I want to be a Christian. I am as far from that as ever. I am only speaking of some possible joy which would draw me from this morass of infection where I have lived till now. But I feel that after overwhelming you with my recriminations,

I have not the right to hide this new feeling from you. You yourself say that even before becoming a Christian, you understood what joy meant through human documents such as the Choruses in Antigone or the Ninth Symphony. Now, I too have loved everything that is beautiful, free, triumphant in art up to the very verge of delirium, so intensely that my whole soul trembled and thrilled. But the exaltation it gave me was a lethal and sombre one, nigher pain than pleasure. Beneath all the beauty I still saw only nothingness. I liked Tristan best of all—oh, how I loved Tristan, with his impenetrable night and the interminable death rattle of despair in his throat! You too, you have felt all this, and know how terrible, for one stricken as I, must be those languorous melodies whose minor seems to be anguished with passion and overcharged with darkness, and whose mournful cadence is lifted up always—always—always to invoke nothingness, death and eternal oblivion. I am almost in tears as I write at the mere recollection of the terror Tristan gave me. It is one of the things that have most confirmed me in my despair. I only tell you all this to show you that the desire for the beautiful, however joyous it be, need not make man be born again, and that all the Ninth Symphony itself might do would be to rend a heart.

Now, perhaps I see something else, something stronger—surer.... But, to return to your letter. How childish it was of me to reproach you with a transition from the subjective to the objective! When from my sentiment of nothingness I pass on and conclude that nothingness exists, what am I doing save objectivizing my own soul? Perhaps at bottom everyone acts the same and cannot act otherwise. Possibly here is the very thing that proves the equivalence of all values, and hence the vanity of them all. And this is to fall into blacker doubt and a more desperate skepticism.

I know that you will take advantage of what I am saying to force me to agree with you that at least I attach no precise value to my negation. Consequently, you will argue, I cannot affirm that nothingness exists. And once again, in your admirable fashion, you will try to prove to me that truth must be real and extrinsic, because it is the necessary complement of our intelligibility—because without it we cannot realize our interior disorder or compare it to the order of the world without. As a matter of fact, I cannot admit a partial disorder. Do your own arguments prove that this disorder is a partial affair? You tell me that "all rhetoric to the contrary notwithstanding, we find that, outside of ourselves, all things are very frankly and fitly adapted to *their* end, which is, to exist and to perpetuate themselves in the plenitude of their nature, and through the mutual concurrence of one with another."

I have two objections to make to this. If they are tenable, they prove disorder to be as complete outside of as within us.

(1) We agree in defining "order" as conformity to certain *ends* and the cooperation of all beings to the same end. But in the present case, what is that "end"? According to your own words it is "to exist and to perpetuate themselves in the plenitude of their nature." But I refuse to call that an "end." Persistence in being does not imply attainment. It is not the same thing as "having an end." I admit the mutual concurrence between created things. But I believe it to be quite void of any objective purpose. I watch its continuous progression, its perpetuation in successive and ever new harmonies; its development even strikes me as being a free one. But I do not see that it is getting anywhere, nor that any goal is proposed for it. Therefore it has no end. Therefore no such thing as an order can exist.

(2) Let us admit that there is such a thing as order (which we cannot do, it seems to me, unless we cease to call mere conformity to one purpose "order"). What tells us that this is not projected upon things by our own intelligence, that it is not, in Kantian terminology, just one of those "forms" under which alone things can be presented to our minds? If so, it merely veils for us the inherent disorder which is the essence of exterior as it is the essence of interior reality. Is it not a little grotesque that order is discoverable everywhere save in ourselves? Is not the discrepancy explained by this fact, that it is just because our knowledge of ourselves is so intimate that we perceive the interior reality by intuition; and know it for what it is, i.e., disorder? When we take off our spectacles we see mistily—because we see truly.

These two objections seem to me a proof that disorder is universal, and consequently to demolish your argument, which is based on the idea that partial disorder is impossible. Nevertheless, to show how little I rely upon them, I don't mind admitting it would be easy for me to turn round and refute them with the help of the admirable critique by Bergson in *l'Evolution Créatrice* of the ideas of nothingness and of disorder. This will convince you what they mean to me, and what small account I make of their demolition by way of philosophy.

I have never accorded, and do not accord now, any demonstrative value to philosophy. The more I know of it, the more I see that it is only a game, the most delightful if only because the most futile and vainest conceivable. What I have just written you is written off-hand. I have recorded it simply to show you that I could, if I wished, demolish your argument and that consequently it has not convinced me. But if it had been conclusively demonstrated to the last hair it would make no difference. My incredulity would remain impregnable as ever. Logic has never meant anything to me. When I think of the fashion in which our ideas are born and the way in which they are affected by association, I could laugh at hearing them accorded the dignity of being named enquiries into the unknown. If something exists—something to which my whole being must respond, I shall not miss it. It will come in a mute, voiceless appeal, through some interior commotion that words are quite powerless to convey. I am listening for it now. At this very moment my whole being is on the alert for it.

What more can I say? I am waiting, I am waiting, with heart and will intact. I do not think I shall be drawn towards Christianity. But something will be changed in me, of that I am sure. Don't regret having spent so much time and trouble over one poor, little, fleeting, instable and elusive soul that slips through your fingers as you grasp it. You see how I abandon my objections every time and yet will not own myself conquered. Up to now it was because I could always think up fresh reasons for not believing. Today it is not even that. I admit whatever you will, I make no fight against your dialectic. And yet I do not yield! How strange such an attitude must seem. And yet I cannot show any other. If I am ever to be brought over it will have to be by some interior force.

I am going to forestall a reproach that you cannot fail to make me, namely, of having misrepresented you a little in my article. I know now that you would not admit owning the views upon predestination that I profess to see, especially in *Mara*. I did not realize the full extent of my error until after the article had gone to press. M. F—— blamed me severely for it. I ask your pardon. I believe the sections to come, upon Original Sin and the Redemption, will repair my fault. Will you tell me if you think I should add a note at the end of the article? If you find any other misreadings, please do not hesitate to tell me, and I will do my best to set them right. I did not send you a copy of *l'Occident* because I knew you would be sure to get it from elsewhere.

Would it be too much to ask you to tell me what you are doing, on what you are at work, and something of your views upon art? This would give me so much pleasure and interest me immensely. You see I am presuming you will be kind enough to write me still!

I will go to Notre Dame and see the Virgin before whom you prayed.

I beg you to believe me, with affectionate respect and passionate devotion.

Yours,

Jacques Rivière

P. S. I think I told you my article would appear in the *Grande Revue.* What happened was that the editor to whom I offered it asked me to send it to him. After a month he sent it back saying that it was very interesting, but that I did not explain you in sufficiently simple language, that I had caught some of your tricks of style (?!), that you were "certainly a very interesting *author* but rather obscure" [yes, for the blind!], that, in any case, he could not give up forty pages of space to a gentleman than whom there were so many more important.

I laughed for both of us.

I do not know whether you get the *Grande Revue.* If you do, you will see a short article by my only friend except yourself called *le Corps de la femme.*† If you read it, I would like you to say something to me about it.

I do not register my letters because I cannot afford the extra postage. I see they seem to reach you regularly, all the same.

Once more believe me most affectionately yours,

J. R.

Dare I ask you to present my respectful regards to Mme. Claudel and to ask for news of your little Marie?

† Alain Fournier: Le Corps de la Femme (*Grande Revue*, December 25, 1907).

To Jacques Rivière

TIEN-TSIN, 11TH JANUARY, 1908

My dear friend,

Your last letter gave me a great deal of pleasure. It was a very nice New Year's gift. Think what you will! You will never possess joy until you approach its source, which is God and Christ. Well! Well! Paris was not built in a day, neither was that mysterious Temple of Jerusalem which the Bible tells us was put together without the sound of axe or hammer.

If you don't mind, we will let philosophy alone for today. All the more so as I see that you don't attach much importance to the objections which you send me. In retaliation, I have made the good resolution of trying to say my rosary every day for your intention. I would be so glad if you would try to acquire this practice also. The rosary is of such tremendous efficacy that even recited without attention on your part, even if you don't believe in it, it will not remain without fruit. It is a marvelous tranquilizer for the soul, and a wonderful key to meditation. If you love me (and you say you do) you will not refuse me a little act of good will, which will unite us day by day in the same thought and the same words.

You ask me for some details about my present life, but there is nothing very remarkable nor very interesting in it. I give half an hour a day to poetry. The rest of my day is devoted to my family and to my duties as magistrate and mayor of the little settlement which I administer. At this moment I am composing the last of four *Grandes Odes*, or psalms, or monologues, in which I resume and am trying to develop the doctrine of my two treatises, mingling with them my theory of the Word, and the incidents of my life past and present. The whole will make a volume which I hope to have printed in the same format and type as the Ode to the Muses. The title is to be "Five Great Odes Followed by a Processional."

As to literary theories, I own frankly that I have not got any. Once upon a time I had certain wise saws, resembling our country proverbs about St. Médard or "rain in the morning," etc. "No overwriting"; "Beware of adjectives," etc. Now I have lost confidence even in these simple rules. The only principle I have left to offer is, "Do whatever you can and as well as you can."

I am still waiting for the articles you mention and which F—— and Jammes have already spoken to me about. You are a very kind young friend indeed, though, so far as benefit to yourself is concerned, you would be much better employed studying something else, the Greeks, the Latins, Shakespeare or Dante. Well, perhaps I can be for you something of what Rimbaud was for me.

My little daughter is a joy! But you are too young to understand the enthusiasms of a father.

Affectionately,

Paul Claudel

To Jacques Rivière
TIEN-TSIN, 28TH JANUARY, 1908

My dear friend,

At last I have the great article, and I will not let false modesty prevent me telling you that it has given me pleasure. For one as little used to literary glory as myself, it is a profound happiness to feel that I am loved and, above all, understood. It is the first time that a detailed study "in form" has been consecrated to my work. For an author, it is a very instructive affair to find himself, as it were, objectivized, and to look at his own reflection in an attentive pair of eyes like yours. You help me very effectively to understand how it comes about that my poetry, my plays and my doctrine, are the fruit of the one aspiration, now pacific, now precipitate. Are you trying to comfort me for the remorse I always feel at having failed to make use of the traditional poetic form? Rhyme and metre always give one's words a character of necessity—of discipline imposed upon them from outside, while my own verse is never anything save a "cry from the heart," a theme composed in solitude, and dependent for its very existence upon the faith and willingness to understand of a friendly reader. Classical verse I consider too rigid and artificial for drama, while in poetry, beyond certain limits, it quickly becomes tiresome and even exasperating (Leconte de Lisle for instance). A regular succession of masculine and feminine rhymes produces a *dazzling* effect like the setting sun seen through a paling as you walk by. What I regret is iambic verse, so pure, so bare, so flexible (see that admirable poem of Catullus, the Marriage of Thetis and Pelion). Among ourselves, Racine and Chénier are the two inimitable masters.

Naturally I understand the limitations of your point of view. But I am rather sorry that you did not point out what I regard as my two main discoveries: *active* sensation and movement independent of local displacement. In other respects your analysis is a marvel of intelligence, even in the passages which for me are the most difficult, (e.g., the Man as Intelligible Victim).

There is one exaggeration which I presume is due to a mere oversight in editing. It is where you say that for me the great, the only sin, is not to remain in one's destiny. For me, as for every Christian, sins are infractions of the Ten Commandments, and their gravity depends absolutely upon matter and intention. But, as an artist, I am at liberty to consider sin from other points of view: either as a symbol, as Our Saviour does in the parable where he praises the unjust steward, or as an application of the text of St. Paul: *Omnia cooperantur in bonum*—"All things work together for good," adding the gloss of St. Augustine, *etiam peccata*, "even sins." For example: the adultery of David, so severely punished, gave us one of those mothers from whom Jesus Christ was descended, as is specifically noted in His genealogy.

I am impatient to see the rest of your article.

I am working now, with a great deal of pleasure, on my Fifth Ode. The idea of one fixed and finite universe, of one sole world inhabited by rational living beings, which I found in Coventry Patmore, and which has been confirmed for me scientifically by Wallace, is, for me, a source of positive illumination. On the other hand, the contrary idea of the infinite, over which Renan gloated so stupidly, as over a precious intellectual conquest, is the dream of barbarous and undeveloped minds. The old geographers did much the same thing. They populated the conjectural portions of their unfinished maps with monsters and prodigies. Christopher Columbus was more than the discoverer of a world: he was the man who made the earth whole again. To the intellect, the *infinite* is everywhere the same abomination and the same scandal. (I am speaking now of the infinite in things which are by their nature finite.) The famous objection: where does the world begin and where does it end? is just as infantile as the denial that it is a sphere because we do not find at times ourselves standing head downward.

In reading a treatise on astronomy—I am thinking of the description of the work of Lagrange on planetary disturbances—one is seized with admiration for the precautions, taken with a precision nothing less than exquisite, that each planet may keep its own orbit. The heavens are a mathematical ecstasy, and the infinite, which is another name for the imperfect, has no place there.

Affectionately,

P. Claudel

To Paul Claudel

PARIS, 22ND FEBRUARY, 1908

Dear and great friend,

I have just received your second letter and your thanks for my article. What a reward! And all the greater because I did not look for it. As long as I had no personal relations with you, I believed I had said what was essential upon you, in terms more or less adequate. But since the beginning of our correspondence doubts had entered my head. I was afraid you might find yourself misrepresented—a thing for which I should never have forgiven myself. Even in re-reading the article after its publication, I came upon more than one place where I had exaggerated or distorted you. The principal one was, just as you say, about the necessity of sin. To tell you the truth I had felt what you tell me before sending in my final copy. But during two years, I had so often re-written it, that a sort of inhibition to alter it again—for which I make no excuse—seized upon me at the last moment. I regret it now.

All the same I do not believe that anyone reading you carefully could get the idea that you consider sin necessary. A man must know Catholicism very badly to be able to misinterpret the *Omnia cooperantur in bonum* in any such sense. It seems to me also that what I go on to say about your views on the punishment of sin, the terrible consequences it entails, on Hell, ought quite sufficiently to correct the passage where careless editing made me misrepresent you.—All the same, if you want me to return to the subject by way of an appendix, I will do so gladly.

It was my intention, in the beginning, to make a great deal of the line: "Evil is in the world, like a slave toiling at a well." There are so many striking things to be said anent this thought that perhaps I shall not be able to resist the temptation of returning to it later. I am also sorry not to have mentioned the *Partage de Midi.* I did not read it until my article was so far advanced that it would have been hard to find a place for comment on it. I also remembered that you had published it privately and might not welcome too much publicity upon it.

I notice that others have not had the same scruple. I wonder whether you think they have anything illuminating to say! I am going to throw off all modesty in turn and tell to you that my article has been the means of introducing you to quite a few people who are already enthusiasts for your work. I hardly know anyone who has not been touched, in one way or another, by the quotations which I used. *And not a single one has accused you of obscurity.* In spite of their literary prejudices, all have felt that they were in contact with something big, and that it behooved them not to speak too loud. You have escaped all such witticisms as for instance pursued Mallarmé (who, by the way, did everything possible to attract them).

Some of my companions at the Normale (five or six at least) have started to read you. At times there is a comic side to it all. One of them followed me about everywhere, asking me: "Why don't you speak of Claudel's sensibility? When are you going to say something about Claudel's sensibility?" I have never succeeded in getting him to define what he called your *sensibility.*

In re-reading your letter I notice that you regret my silence on active sensation and movement independent of local displacement. On the first subject, as you perceive yourself, the limitations of my point of view prevented me from being more explicit. I was considering the world in its totality as *becoming* and was not greatly concerned at the fashion in which individuals perceived circumambient forms by their contours. I understood the argument and realized its importance. But space compelled me to make more than one sacrifice.

As to movement independent of local displacement (I imagine you refer to interior vibration and to the inversion that takes place when energy finds itself hindered of expansion by the limits of its container), I said something on page 170. But perhaps I was not sufficiently emphatic. If you wish, I will deal with it further in an appendix. Tell me if these are the only two questions that you find have been treated inadequately.

Thank you for what you tell me about your work. With what impatience I shall wait your Odes! Divagations upon the infinite, and that species of ecstasy because the sky has neither top nor bottom have always wounded me as an indelicacy might, I think myself it is not so much, as you say, a childish and barbaric notion, as a concept of the sham-scientist, whose head has been turned by astronomical formulae. It is just like believing the world is an admirable thing because no one knows by which end to take hold of it. So far as I know, the primitive peoples never imagined a world without bounds. They conceived of every human habitation as having four walls and a roof.—This is in direct contradiction with what I said in my *Meditation on the Extreme West.* But I have committed many stupidities in the course of my short life, and this was one of the worst. I wrote it off-hand and misled by I know not what evil spirit. It has taught me to think twice and more than twice now before I speak.

I have tried to pray as you ask me, if only so as to be with you. But I have lost the habit so completely that I don't get very far. I promise you, however, to do my very utmost. But remember what a child I really am, in spite of my twenty-two years. I spend my life oscillating between extremes of despair and exaltation. There are moments when I have the very taste of death in my mouth, when I know that all is over, that there is nothing more to expect. This mood can last four days, that are like as many centuries.

Suddenly I rise—I soar: I am strong, I command. I draw in great breaths, pride expands my chest. Until the next fall! When I am down—down—I feel the need to cry: My God! My God! To throw myself upon my knees, to form words with my lips. But no sooner cured, I am again incapable of any sort of devotion. Once more I feel nothing but the tempest of my force and that admirable lightness of spirit which is a species of ecstasy.

But I promise you faithfully to do all within my power—and that is very little—to pray with you.

I pass now to a very different subject, and you will have to forgive me the incoherence of this letter.—I mean what you say about Rimbaud.—How happy I am to see that he has meant something to you as well! My friend, Fournier (I have spoken of him to you already), and myself both thought we detected some reminiscences of him in your *Connaissance de l'Est*. Isn't this true about him—the great terrible poet: *People don't speak of him because he frightens them?* I would like you to tell me what you think of him.

Possibly I shall make up my mind to put together some rather amusing ideas that I have in my head under the title *Introduction to a Metaphysical Study of Dreams.* While saying certain things that are very serious, it would be a wonderful chance to poke fun at professors of philosophy in general.

* * * * *

I have already afforded you so many opportunities for forgiveness that you will not change now and refuse to pardon me this budget of trivialities and incoherences.

Please believe in the very deep and very respectful admiration of your insupportable young friend,

Jacques Rivière

To Jacques Rivière

TIEN-TSIN, 12TH MARCH, 1908

My dear friend,

I have this moment received your letter and the number of the *l'Occident* containing the second section of your article on me, and I answer you immediately so as to be sure of forgetting nothing. Like Dickens's Mr. Grewgious, I proceed point by point.

I am very proud of your article and very much pleased at what is really the first analytical study ever written on my work. You have succeeded in making clear quite a number of things in what to many people (perhaps even to myself) seemed inextricable confusion. Naturally I take due account of the omissions which any constructive work demands. Even so, there are three remarks that I am compelled to make, although it is only to the first that I attach any great importance.

To say that "the soul does not differ substantially from God" would be plain heresy. The very substance of the soul is its difference from God. How one simplex can differ from another is something we have still to learn. It is one of the points where my own theory is incomplete and as yet presents only what stone-masons call "corbels." (The same applies to the distinction between the soul and matter.) On the topic of the simplicity of the soul, I have followed the classical Thomist theory. What would be interesting to ascertain would be just to what degree simplicity excludes combination. For example: God is simplex yet three persons in One. Today my own tendency is rather to regard simplicity as an abnormal element, artificial, violent and even illusory. Nothing exists without certain inter-relations.

In the quotation you use (from page 269, seventh and following lines), my own language was none too clear. The last encyclical comes to remind us that between God and man the relation is one of congruity and not of necessity. Otherwise we should find ourselves in full pantheism.

By movement independent of local displacement, I mean more particularly the alternation of tension and relaxation, action and force—in a word, the substantial vibration into which, after death, complete knowledge will be inserted, very much as perception now reaches us through the vibration of our senses. Life after death will be a conscious informing and auto-production in one image, an exquisite differing from God, seen face to face.

On the doctrine of sin, I have often had the following objection made to me in conversation: "Confession is too convenient! A mere *mea culpa* suffices to clear the conscience of a whole series of sins and of the evils which they have set in motion." Perhaps: but it is consoling to consider that sin may produce good results as well as bad ones. What the *avowal* in confession clears us of is our personal *responsibility.*

* * * * *

What you say on the subject of the infinite is excellent. I hope and trust that well-intentioned minds will soon be freed of the frightful incubus that has weighed on previous generations. Kant says that space cannot be limited by non-space. This is a pure sophism. The position of any unknown point can only be indicated by its relation to other known points. Once its position with reference to these is determined, the problem is completely solved. A "limit" is only a scission between two homogeneous parts: where there is no longer homogeneity but negation, there can be no limit. It is the same old Kantian confusion between different categories of knowledge, which denies all value to sensible perception because it is not rational perception. To each order its proper instruments! Do we refuse to trust our ears because we cannot use them to detect odors?

The same thing as regards the infinitely divisible. A straight line can be cut into an infinity of morsels; not so a child, nor a triangle, which are indivisible, nor even motion, but only the line, which is its motionless symbol. All Kant's antinomies are based upon the faculty of the mind to picture to itself the act of adding, and adding, and adding—unit upon unit—*ad infinitum.*

Of all the influences which have been brought to bear upon me, Rimbaud was the chief. Others, notably Shakespeare, Eschylus, Dante and Dostoievsky, have been my masters and have taught me the secrets of my craft. But Rimbaud alone has had that influence which I term seminal and generative, and which makes me really believe that in the spiritual, as in the physical, order, there is such a thing as actual fatherhood. I shall never forget the morning in June, 1886, on which I bought the slim issue of *la Vogue* which contained the first part of *Illuminations.* For me the word "illumination" was not too strong. At last I felt myself breaking away from that hideous world of the Taines, the Renans and our other nineteenth-century molochs, from that prison-house, that hideous mechanism, governed from top to bottom by laws whose perfect inflexibility was rendered infinitely horrible by the fact that they could neither be learnt nor taught. (Automata have always inspired me with a sort of hysterical horror.) At last I had a revelation of the supernatural. Here was genius in its sublimest and purest form, like an inspiration whose source it is futile to seek.

* * * * *

We have been writing to one another now for a year, and it seems a fitting time to strike a sort of balance of our relations. You have brought me keen joy—what author would not love to have his thought comprehended and studied as by you?—but still keener misgivings. I hope that our correspondence has been profitable to yourself in the same way. God likes to enter and dwell in a well-ordered house. But the greatest enemy of the Holy Ghost is the secret thought: "After all, I am worth something!"

Since you are a caller upon my Virgin of Notre Dame, tell her that I want to leave Tien-Tsin, where I am bored to death with my municipal council, and three journalists. The most disgusting of the trio I have just been obliged to expel.

Sincerely,

P. Claudel

The very surest method of softening your heart would be to visit the poor. Why don't you join some Conference of St. Vincent de Paul? To begin with, it would be an excellent medicine for self-love. Besides this, you would be helping your suffering brethren, and performing a practical and effective act of love towards God's image on earth which would not be left without its reward.

To Paul Claudel

EASTER SUNDAY, 19TH APRIL, 1908

My dear great friend,

I am a little late in replying to you. You will see, when you have read this letter, how many distractions I can offer as an excuse.

I have many things to say in reply to your letter. First of all, you criticise me for having, in my article, spoken of a confusion of substance as between the soul and God. I admit that no passage in your work authorized me to attribute this idea to you, and that consequently I am to blame.

All the same, I would like to ask you whether this confusion is not implicit in Christianity itself, or, at any rate, in Christian theology. The very admirable frankness with which you tell me that upon this point your system is as yet unfinished, confirms me in my opinion, which first came to me when I was studying Fénelon's *Théodicée* for a philosophical paper I was writing. You know, of course, that Fénelon, his life long, had all he could do to keep his footing upon the brink of pantheism to which his doctrines were inevitably leading him. I believe (and indeed tried to say so in my monograph) that his famous quietism had a good deal to do with this tendency in his philosophical system. But, on thinking the matter over, I finally began to ask myself whether it did not come from further back, and derive from an idea that is of the essence of Christianity.

Fénelon (or so it seems to me), was not alone in attributing the perfection of the creature to God, tracing it back to God, and renewing it through God. Christian theology conceives God as everything, the creature as nothing—I mean in the order of perfection. But, according to another theory, perfection is synonymous with being—is being's *self.* All being is good; all goodness is some form of being; the infinitely good is the infinite Being. To be good, and to exist at all are synonymous.—Hence, if one refers all perfection to God, one refers all being to Him as well.

It cannot be retorted that this association is merely the designation of a common origin. I hold that it must be understood as a real attribution of this *being* to God, as an affirmation that He alone possesses it actually—that this being is in Him.

Else, what is the meaning of the words "emanation," "communication," used of His infinite perfection? Can the goodness of God, which is His being, be partially subtracted from Him, and installed temporarily in individuals distinct from Himself? I don't think so. Participation in God's being is necessarily a confusion of substance with Him, since nothing can be taken away from His perfection without diminishing its infinity, and consequently depriving Him of His quality as God. When you attribute to the Creator all the perfection of His creatures, you preclude any substantial distinction between them.

Possibly you will say that the identification of existence with perfection is not an article of faith and hence, that one can invest the perfection of finite beings in God without investing their existence in Him. In that case, I would like to ask you what existence can be if not perfection, and what perfection can be if not existence. If existence be not perfection, then, in giving it to His creatures, God has given them something bad, and they are no longer responsible for the evil with which this state inspires them. On the other hand, if perfection be not existence, what is there in it real or positive? Its finiteness? But in God, infinite perfection is precisely infinity of being. There is nothing positive that is not existence. Now perfection is necessarily something positive. Hence perfection is existence.

Existence and perfection, then, being one and the same thing, when we refer the perfection of the creature back to God (and we are forced to recognize it as an actual possession) we identify his existence with the Divine Being. It follows that the tendency of Christian theology is towards pantheism.

This is confirmed by facts. I note, on the one hand, the extremely daring expressions of the Fathers and Mystics on the subject of confusion of substance, e.g. (*Perit quodam modo humana meus et fit divina.* St. Augustine, *Nihil amare in homine nisi Deum.* Idem, etc.), and on the other hand your own hesitancy on the question.

The explanation which you suggest of a distinction between the soul and God by reading a deeper implication into the notion of simplicity, is attractive. But how, even admitting that the simplex is compatible with composition, does this prove, after what I have said, that the soul and God are separate? The simplicity of the former may be the result of a different correlation to the correlation which makes the simplicity of the Divine. This does not alter the fact that, by referring to God the perfection which it comprises, we end by referring to God its actual existence.

To be quite fair, I don't mind admitting that a grave objection, though a very old one, can be made to my line of reasoning. It can be argued that God enjoys His perfection intensively but not extensively, and His existence, consequently, in the same fashion.

But, first of all, when the perfection of the creature is attributed to Him, it is the perfection of such and such a creature, individually—it is the aggregate of limited perfections of all beings actually in existence—hence, extensive perfection. If not—if we content ourselves by saying that the perfection of such and such an individual has its model, its correspondence, in the intensive and indivisible perfection of God, to what shall we attribute this particular and individual perfection, distinct from that of God? Has the being conferred it on himself? Or, if it comes from God, where, outside of Himself, has He taken it? Where was it existent and how did He create it without subtracting its essence from Himself?

It is not even clear to me how existence can be possessed intensively and not extensively. The distinction between an extensive and an intensive totality only exists in a qualificative sense. But existence is a thing whose maximum can only be a numerical total, in other words, the aggregate of all existence whatsoever.

I stop here. My intention has been merely to divert myself by proposing a few reflections to you. I believe they could be carried on *ad infinitum*, without arriving at any positive result. I think I have said enough to prove my point, which is, that Christianity puts itself in peril when it attempts to rely on philosophy for its proofs.

This abstract notion of God, from which the Cartesian theology of the seventeenth century affected to derive all truth, is, in reality, an inexhaustible source of contradictory statements. More and more I am led to see that there is but one way of representing God. I see an old bearded man seated among thunder-clouds. Or Jesus in the crib, visible to the eyes, sensible to the touch, and opening His arms to me. It is for this very thing—for having created and kept before us a human, concrete conception of God, ever-present and easily adorable, that non-theological Christianity is so marvelous.

Only prigs or fools deny religion because they find it too concrete. Nothing shows smallness of mind so much as offence at being asked to believe in a History of God. The iconoclast is a malefactor whose cranium has been blown empty by his habit of abstract thought.

I believe, I understand, I love only that which I can touch, something that is apprehensible by my senses, that can lie under my hand and leave a taste on my lips. A man must be pretty confused in his mind, and very ignorant indeed, to believe that a method and a few concepts can procure him anything tangible. No one who has played with ideas, and knows how entrancing a sport it is to model them, destroy them, transform them into one another, can ever believe that they have any correspondence with reality. I will wager to take any idea whatsoever and merely by taking advantage of its essential plasticity, to construct any system you please, or even two mutually contradictory systems, out of it. It is appalling to think that people can busy themselves with philosophy and not realize what a fickle, wanton, undependable and futile game they are playing.

* * * * *

Yes, I have read Wallace. He is wonderful for the demonstration which, little by little, takes root and grows out of his immense accumulation of facts. But of what use to me is all his argumentation, this confirmation through telescope and camera? Is there anyone who does not perceive at a glance that this world is an accomplished fact, that it is composed like a poem, controlled in its every movement by a central intelligence? Can I not reach out to the furthest stars when I wish, since it is them I see and not others? Those who need Wallace to make them believe in the unity of the universe are like people who need a photograph to help them believe in a landscape.

Nothing is proved to me except by contact.

* * * * *

It is both a duty and a pleasure to me to inform you, before I close this letter, that I am engaged to be married. I know this is going to surprise you, and even make you a little uneasy for my sake. But I know so well what I am doing! I feel strong and happy. I have fought, resisted, tried to do violence to myself. All was of no use! Now I am at peace because I am a "lost man." Do you remember the torments about which I wrote you, the remedies I told you I was seeking—and then the time I told you I was experiencing a joy? That was the moment when I surrendered!

Now my worries seem nearly over. There are so many things I see clearly now. I am cured of my literary gestures. A host of intolerable desires have taken flight. I no longer look at my own reflection nor preen my feathers. Yet, suddenly, I seem to understand myself better.

Yes, I feel strong and happy. And I believe that this simpler attitude toward myself which has permitted me to find something in myself that rang true, is largely your work. I owe you both love and gratitude. Who knows?—Perhaps before the end you may have changed me completely.

Assuring you of my most profound and respectful affection.

Jacques Rivière

To Jacques Rivière

TIEN-TSIN, 11TH MAY, 1908

My dear friend,

Your reasoning proceeds from a confusion in logic between "some" and "all"—in other words between similarity and identity. *Some being* cannot be *all-being*, for the latter, insofar as it suffers division or separation, ceases to be all-being. The difference is radical and substantial. The logical object is determined by the points where its limits are reached. Now God is perfect. Therefore there is no point at all where actual perfection does not exist, that is to say where there is any admixture of potentiality with action. Just as there can be only one God, so there cannot be more than one perfection, the very property of perfection being to preclude partition.

But, if man is not God, he is *of* God, and God's image. It is in this sense that we even can say he *is* God, just as the first glance at certain pictures makes us say: "This is a Rubens!" or "This is a Manet!" The parallel is inexact because the artist separates himself from his work when he leaves it, whereas the creation is a work upon which the Creator never ceases to operate. He gives us life as a mother gives it to her son, from whom, nevertheless, she remains different. He is the source of our vital power. Dedicated to its sustenance as to some secret objective, He lets Himself be drawn upon incessantly. We do not share His perfection, since Unity cannot be divided. But from contact with Him we conceive our individual perfection. Nevertheless we are something *of* God, a special act of

His will, very much as though some motif of Beethoven should take on an existence of its own. (Hence, the enormity of evil and impiety—the defilement which we inflict upon the divine image.) And, being *of* God, we are also *in* God, according to the phrase of the apostle. *In Deo vivimus et movemus et sumus*: In God we live and move and have our being. It is, moreover, an article of faith that God is everywhere, since everything is His work.

This idea of a division and sharing of the essence of God is a relic of the false conceptions of the nineteenth century, with its notion of substance as inert and of matter as indifferent.

In strict truth, no being endures division. What then shall we say of *the* Being par excellence?—Who is not only such by abstraction and retrenchment of all sensible qualities, but whose perfection is the modality and necessary condition of all being.

These, at any rate, are my views upon the subject, and I believe they have in them a large proportion of settled theology. We can affirm the substantial difference between man and God, between imperfect and perfect. Naturally I cannot demonstrate it to you. Such a demonstration would require a simultaneous view of the two substances side by side, which is impossible in this life.

This brings me to another part of your letter, and one which I do not much like. I mean the airy tone with which you speak of the highest faculties of our intelligence, as though they were meant for nothing better than our amusement and recreation. The wretched Renan has written any number of drolleries on this subject, and a host of despicable scribblers have followed in his wake, among whom I hate to see you mingle even for a moment, any more than I would care to see a clean-living lad among a rascally group of students. Our very limited intelligence does not afford us clear views upon everything. But this is no reason for mistrusting her in the sphere where she exercises her legitimate functions. This waste of and contempt for the gifts of God, even His most admirable, fills me with horror. To believe that our intelligence is only good enough to divert us is very much like saying that the best use of poetic imagination is to write parnassian sonnets or *revues.* The truth of the matter is that our intellectual faculties cannot be used properly without a method and a deeply sincere and sober mind. Think of the infinity of precautions that astronomers take to ensure the accuracy of their instruments. The scholastic writers of old days had an admirable system of discipline, built up upon the principles of Aristotle. Since its disappearance, we have fallen into the realm of fiction, and into a chaos of hasty and petulant affirmations, amid which it is small wonder that a young man cannot keep his head.

I believe that we can conceive a much better idea of God the Father than that of an old man with a long beard. It is just at this point that the holy frontiers of the spirit commence. It is here that a man, laying aside his senses as Moses cast off his sandals before the burning bush, or, like Jesus, leaving behind Him His three apostles, may pray a little afar off, "a stone's-throw" away, and trust Himself to nothing save His heart and intelligence. It is here that metaphysical awe and terror, the "ecstatic aphasia" that Plotinus speaks of, begin. As a matter of fact, the notion we have of God, however hard we may find it to express, is far more poignant and intense than that which we have of any concrete and familiar object whatsoever.

I have just room to add sincere congratulations on your forthcoming marriage, both to you and your *fiancée*, with heartfelt wishes for your happiness in the future. Why do you tell me you are a "lost man"? All that has befallen you is that, in your life, order and duty are from now on to play an increasing part, and I perceive a design of God at which I rejoice. My hope is that the partial order will lead you to the supreme.

Please convey my respects to your *fiancée* and believe me sincerely your friend,

P. Claudel

To Paul Claudel

PARIS, 27TH JUNE, 1908

My dear friend,

Let me tell you at once how greatly my *fiancée* and myself appreciate your good wishes and congratulations. I assure you that they mean a great deal to us both. When I told you I was a "lost man," it was a joke, and only to make you understand how fully I realized I was a saved one.

I have no fresh arguments to oppose to your refutation of my pantheist dialogue, though I own to you that mental sluggishness keeps me musing upon the old theme. It is upon another subject—the gratuity of the intelligence—that I wish to reply to you now.

I might almost say that I have never received a letter from you which has not been, in one way or another, a reproach, and which has not revealed to me some secret insincerity I did not suspect. Each time I have rebelled and have borne you a grudge for a few hours. But each time, also, I have been forced to own that you were right.

Nevertheless, upon this last point, the aptness of your criticism is largely due to the fact that I explained myself badly. And I insist upon maintaining certain things, if only because I have noted, and note without ceasing, that they are an inherent part of me.

I must continue, for instance, to believe that rational thought is not an instrument for veritable knowledge, that it is not directed toward the discovery of the real; in a word, that it has no objectivity.

I do not say this through any affectation of skepticism, after the manner of Renan, nor in the character of an aesthete and dilettante. I would be horrified to find myself confounded with the "despicable scribblers" of whom you speak. But I must be guided by experience. I observe in myself the fashion in which ideas are born. I note that their origin is purely internal, that an argument arises, grows and takes on form, very much as a composition might arise, grow and take on form in the brain of a painter. Even when it is a question of expounding the ideas of someone else, my analysis and criticism *take shape in me* in just the same fashion. Here is an instance. When I was preparing my thesis on Fénelon, it happened that I had a chapter in my head, entirely laid out except for one or two of its sections. As I walked about quietly with my mind concentrated and, as it were, *pressing upon* these empty spaces, an idea was conceived and born in each which was the very one I needed, and which, when developed, had all the air of being necessitated by the context and of interpreting exactly one side of the doctrine I was expounding. So much so that the two professors who corrected my papers praised the tightness of my exposition and the solidity of the whole argument.

If this can be so when the case is one of criticism, what is likely to happen when construction and system are in question? I stand face to face with my invention as a painter stands before his canvas, half-closing his eyes and adding a touch of his brush here, a touch there. I see blank spots, I excite two or three ideas which I hope will fill them, and of these I choose the ones which will harmonize best with the rest of the picture. How, I ask you, am I to believe in the objectivity of a method when I know its tricks and turns so well—or in the truth of a play at whose every rehearsal I have assisted behind the scenes? I repeat to you that with ideas, a man can do anything he pleases, proving and disproving at his will.

You may object that, if I doubt the value of my own ideas, it is because I have not submitted them, as did the scholastics, to the rules of logic from their very inception. But who is to guarantee the value of these rules? Who is to persuade me that by exact reasoning I shall attain the truth? Even the scholastics were not prepared to confound the form of logic with its matter. They believed that the logical machine could operate with the utmost precision without necessarily producing anything. Once again—nothing intrinsic can assure me of the reality of thought. And observation forces me to maintain that thought takes shape without any objective in view. It is only in a species of mirage that its content is projected outside of myself at all, just as it is possible to consider the exteriority of sensation as an hallucination.

I could, if I would, demonstrate that all the great systems of philosophy have been conceived by their authors purely as artistic compositions. The metaphysics of Plato, Descartes, Malebranche and Spinoza could be drawn with a pencil and paper. You will say it is just because their genesis can be so plainly indicated that we know their doctrines are false. But how am I to be made believe that the Christian metaphysic was planned and constructed any differently?

It may well be these justifications of my apparent dilettantism strike you as inadequate. If so, the real reason lies in that species of doubt, of secret clairvoyance, which stops me from taking what I think seriously. This doubt is the very fibre of my mind, its essential constituent. From childhood, in the face of every opinion I heard uttered, I asked: Why do you think this? And I was always able to find reasons very, very different from those which were vouchsafed me. What I found admirable in Nietzsche is that he shows us the source of a host of affirmations, even scientific ones, which are given out as impersonal—even as dictated by the facts themselves—while, in reality, they are only so many views, derived from practice and held without any particular objective. The only legitimate sense in which intelligence can be affirmed as objective is by explaining, with Kant, that it creates its own object. But what does that objectivity signify, if there is nothing true except the noumenon?

Please do not be indignant with me for this tissue of impieties. Remember that I could only be in accord with you upon the adaptability of the intelligence to its end, if I shared your faith. Faith in individual matter can only exist if one possesses *the* central and vital Faith. Either the one or the other! What disgusts, or rather, amuses me, is to see people who have any religion at all, the prey to every variety of credulity and charlatanry, to see professors of philosophy quite persuaded, in spite of the innumerable bankruptcies that have gone before, that they can arrive at truth through sheer reason and that no previous adhesion of the heart to "mysteries" is needed.

I would add this: Even if it is granted that intelligence is only play, the implication does not seem to me so grave a downfall as you think. Play is still the best thing there is in our lives. What are the arts if not so much play? When is it so necessary to be strong and free as when playing? It is during play that the being gathers itself together, like a beast crouching, and lets itself go in one movement, like the same beast leaping. It is at play alone that man finds his veritable unity, because it is only at play that he flings off his complexities, his inhibitions, his fears and his scruples, and becomes a gesture, a rush, a force set free. It is when playing and not when busy on his miserable tasks, obscure, vain and useless as the daily sweeping of a courtyard by a *concierge*, that he is doing something worth while.

Answer me, please, and do not withdraw your friendship, which is very dear to me. I beg you to accept the assurance of my humble and very profound affection.

Jacques Rivière

To Paul Claudel

PARIS, 29TH NOVEMBER, 1908

Dear and great friend,

For two whole months I have put off writing you, distracted as I have been by a thousand and one petty tasks, and, above all, undecided whether your silence after my last letter may not mean that my little subtleties and quibblings have at last been too much for your tireless patience. Neither can I explain why I did not tell you of my joy at the birth of your son, which, like everything concerning you, came home to me very closely. I am still wondering why I did not write you when I read of it.

Somehow I shudder when I think of the mass of stupidity, bombast and nullity that you have received from me. I would give a great deal to feel sure that you had destroyed all my letters.

What am I to tell you now? I am no nearer Christianity, no more courageous than before, I have no better right than before to believe myself your friend. But I still want you, in spite of what you esteem my weaknesses and errors, to keep a little of the affection that you seemed to have for me.

I am too tired after all the work I have been through for my fellowship examination (all the more important to me as it is the condition of my marriage) to be able to write you a very interesting letter.

During the past vacation I have been giving a good deal of thought to the sort of thesis I shall write. Even to forecast it gave me a fever. But it will probably displease you, and it will be bad enough for you to read it when it is written.

Three months ago I sent my *Introduction to a Metaphysic of Dreams*, of which I think I spoke to you, to the *Mercure*. I have heard nothing since and cannot even find out if it has been rejected.

Have you read *The Shield of the Zodiac*, by Suarès? It is admirable, yet terrible and insupportable at the same time, one of those books which one can neither live with nor tear oneself away from. Its author seems to me the only antagonist worthy to answer you.

Did you get the *Grande Revue* which I sent you? There was an essay in it by my friend Fournier, rather old now and already a little disowned.

Please excuse this untidy letter. I only send it so as to get an answer in which you tell me that you forgive me.

Sincerely and respectfully your friend,

Jacques Rivière

To Jacques Rivière

TIEN-TSIN, 19TH DECEMBER, 1908

My dear friend,

I have just got your little letter. The friendship of which you assure me makes me very happy; please believe that I keep mine for you. If I left you without an answer it was because the utility of our correspondence was no longer apparent to me. When I wrote you before, it was with the brotherly hope of doing you good, and not to enter upon a series of barren philosophical controversies, for which I have neither the taste nor the facility. I perceive that you have emerged from the period of crisis through which the élite of each generation pass in their turn, with the usual result. Do not regret the confidences which you have made to me and of which I feel myself honored to have been made the recipient. Today you seem to me to be inclining rather on the side of Renan and de Gourmont than towards mine. I am the wrong person to send an apologetic on "play" to. I am not an emancipated spirit; I am a simple and serious man: as an artist I despise virtuosity and fail to understand facetiousness. From Voltaire and Anatole France, the sneer has always seemed to me the stigmata of reprobation. From the moment a man is possessed by hatred for God, he is no longer able to repress his laughter.

I knew X——for four years and often saw him when I was passing through Paris. Desperately sick at heart and suffering intensely, he gave me, like the majority of those which have opened their hearts to me, only a bitter consciousness that I was powerless to help. Art is but a pale counterfeit of sanctity. The vegetation its tepid rays bring to life has no roots and is ephemeral as that of the gardens of Adonis. Its books are full of talent, but *cui bono*? Have not all the *great* writers of the century which has just passed away sufficiently reiterated the vanity of life, the illusion of joy, the certainty of nothing save damnation and despair? Let them eat of the bread of their art—feed on the dream which they have found so full of savour. For me—I believe in a good God and in a *profitable* life, where it matters a great deal which road a man takes.

Goodbye, my dear friend. I grasp your hand affectionately, and on the threshold of another year, wish you all success and happiness in the life upon which you are entering.

P. Claudel

To Jacques Rivière

FRENCH CONSULATE AT TIEN-TSIN, 20TH DECEMBER, 1908

My dear friend,

Hardly had I put my last letter in the mail than I began to reproach myself because it exaggerated a certain aspect of the feeling that I have for you. One of the drawbacks of my "clerical" temperament is a sort of jealousy that I feel towards people upon whom I had hoped to be a good influence. I firmly hope that God will forgive me this, and one day make Himself clear to you without any help from me. Already He is sending you one of the greatest graces a man can receive, that of "necessity." But I was placing such great hopes in you. You are about to be a professor and a writer to boot. How grave a responsibility! I hope at least that you will never let any portion of that burden with which you have been nearly overwhelmed fall upon the shoulders of the young people whose guide you are going to become in turn. It is so easy to demolish and to doubt! It is so hard to create and to build up!

Begging you to present my regards to your *fiancée*, I remain, affectionately yours,

P. Claudel

P. S. I have just sent the MSS of *Five Odes* to *l'Occident.* But it will probably be some time before they are printed.

To Paul Claudel

PARIS, 17TH JANUARY, 1909

My dear big friend,

You had indeed been cruel to me in your first letter. Naturally, it never once occurred to me that you were not in the right. But I would have preferred you to be just a little in the wrong. Your second letter did me good and gave me the courage to answer you.

I promise faithfully not to annoy you with my philosophic discussions any more. But if you knew how far from "play" I am already! If you knew how unjust it was to throw me to one side with Renan and de Gourmont!—de Gourmont, that wretched physiologist! Perhaps I justified your comparison by appearing a skeptic. But my skepticism is something passionate, blind and tense. Can you dream that I have any desire to act the dilettante? At the bottom of my heart, possession is what I crave most and I am driven incessantly towards possessions which I believe to be definite ones. Is it my fault if I am forced to conclude that they are not? It is my disappointments, my continual misadventures that make my skepticism. If I ever seemed satisfied with it, you may be sure this was only irony.

There are moments when I am inwardly persuaded that I shall become a Christian. How I cannot imagine, but I feel it. So do not let us go different ways. Let me feel that you are never too far off. This will cost you only a few brief letters from time to time, and, if you come to France in June as you say, permission to come and see you.

I don't know what you will think of the book I have in my head, once it is written. Doubtless it will displease you because, though it will be near Christianity, it will be outside of it and even trying to discount it. But, whatever you think of it, it will help you to understand that a violent effort to believe, made spontaneously and passionately, can be allied to what I term desperate clarity of vision. Believe me, once more! My doubt and my plastic conception of ideas, so far from being an intellectual amusement, are the result of a renunciation that is forced on me. It is because I believe they have nothing to do with truth that I use them as elements of art. In any case, I take no pleasure in the game. I have something else to think of.

I saw Mithouard the other day. He told me he had received your *Odes*, but that he was going to have grave difficulties in printing them on account of his small supply of type. It seems that we are going to be made to wait some time (I say *we* because there is quite a little group of us now who love your work).

M. F——, whom I saw during the few days I spent in Bordeaux, told me that you had written him saying that Jules Romains had talent. He is a student at Normal School, and is preparing for his fellowship with me. He is an interesting man. But very touchy about his anonymity (Jules Romains is a pen-name). Even those who are in the secret never refer to it with him.

The *Nouvelle Revue Française* suspended publication after its first issue. André Gide, who was one of the principal organizers, told me that he didn't like the first number, but hopes to start again shortly with a new staff of collaborators.

You will call what I am sending you a "little letter" again. Forgive me. What I want, even if you judge it useless to answer me, is to go on speaking to you from time to time, so that, if I am ever brought nearer you, I shall know where to find you and can depend on your support. I write badly because I am tired. But you understand me. I beg you, dear friend, to believe as ever in my profound and humble friendship,

Jacques Rivière

To Jacques Rivière
4TH FEBRUARY, 1909

My dear friend,

Don't let my bouts of ill-temper worry you. If I treat you so badly, it is because I am very fond of you, think of you a great deal, and consequently, am sometimes vexed and impatient with you. I have so much compassion for young people who, like myself, have had to take their first steps amid the pestilential darkness of university education! It was first principles that failed our generation. Even for me, who received such graces, who am a thousand times surer of the truth of the Catholic religion than that the sun will rise tomorrow—as sure as if I had seen the Saviour with my own eyes, and whose faith was as complete at the first moment of conversion as it is today—four years were needed merely to conquer human respect. So write me whatever you like. So long as I can believe that my letters are agreeable or useful, it will always be a joy for me to answer. I shall be in France at the end of July. Not for long, I think. Your black Paris winter with its sulphurous atmosphere terrifies me.

Gide asked me to write for his new review. I sent him my *Hymn to the Blessed Sacrament*, one of those I wrote to lighten the labor upon my new play; a painful task, as it always is when one's whole scheme and manner have to be changed. At present the timbers of my new barque are cracking and straining under the helmsman's hand.

I have just met a most attractive soul, one M. L——, a convert, brought up at the Cairo School, who became a Catholic after a long stay in the East. Curiously enough, the impulse for conversion came to him while studying the life of a Mohammedan who was burnt to death about the year 1000 for having become a Christian. A few ashes in the folds of an old manuscript was the soil in which this rose took root and grew! I receive the most saintly letters from him, which fill me with joy. You don't know what it is to love Christ, and to see Him in every book or newspaper that you receive, insulted, scoffed at or hypocritically praised. How one's heart is drawn to the few kindred souls who still love the poor abandoned Saviour!

Sincerely,

P. Claudel

To Paul Claudel

BORDEAUX, 7TH APRIL, 1909

My dear great friend,

After having implored you so to keep up our correspondence, what excuse am I to give you for my long silence? A flock of distractions, the chief and the most troublesome of which was my work at the Sorbonne, obliged me to put off answering you till the Easter holidays.

And I had so many things to talk to you about. Now perhaps I shall forget some of them.

First of all: I am so sorry to see the production of *la Jeune Fille Violaine* put off again. I have often imagined what your plays would be like on the stage and have longed to see them acted. Doubtless it will be hard to get the perfect direction and acting necessary for them more than for any others. Supposing this realized, I believe the impression produced on the public would be tremendous. Up to now this public has not been exactly glutted with good things, and ignorance (as long as it is a healthy ignorance) presents no obstacle. I have always refused to concede that some of your plays were more adapted for the stage than others. My opinion has been that one and all cried out for a dramatic presentation, and that, of all our playwrights, you were even in the conventional use of the word the most dramatic. Anyhow, you won't have long to wait now, and as soon as one's personal anxieties are over, people of good will are never hard to find. Among one group of young men I witnessed a positive outburst of enthusiasm when they heard of Bour's offer. What were they not prepared to do to ensure the success of *la Jeune Fille Violaine!*

I have read your Hymn to the Blessed Sacrament. How dare I even speak of it? The triumph of certitude throughout it came home to me like a reproach. I was especially moved by the lines:

> *We too, my God, see that You are alone and abandoned of men,*
> *Like some greybeard in the midst of these vagrants of a day, these frivolous youths busied with vanity.*

Elsewhere, however, I was troubled to find myself no longer seized by the old transports. I felt as though some vision had gone from me, and that my interest had become that of a spectator from outside. My vexation was all the greater because I had to own that I have ceased to deserve the old emotion. André Lhote, the young painter of whom M. F——has spoken to you, felt the same. We said: "It must be because we are no longer Christians that we cannot understand the awful beauty of this Hymn." The beginning, however, is not yet beyond my reach, and I thrill to it as I did to *les Muses* and *l'Arbre.*

In the course of my philosophical reading I have been studying the stoics, and have acquired a positive hatred of their cowardly system of ethics. It would be no disaster if its influence had died out. Unfortunately, at every instant in our contemporary appreciations of men and things, I find signs that the values it invented still survive. I have a horror of the impassive attitude toward life. Yet for many it is the supreme virtue. This frugality of feeling, this fashion of reducing one's emotional expenses to inanition, this refusal to fulfil oneself, to consume oneself, this pride in persisting as an isolated and intact entity, is odious to me. I have committed a good many faults, and if I ever become a Christian I shall have plenty of sins to confess. But at least I have never spared myself. Never has anything passed before me without affecting me strongly, or left me without taking away with it as it went, something of my love and of my life, or without leaving its imprint on my body. It is true I believe all this consumption of myself vain. I cannot see that it does good to anyone. But I do not hesitate before it. I could not spend myself more willingly if I believed in an eternal reward. It is precisely this moral code of fulfilment, of consumption, which attracted me so much to your plays, especially to *Partage de Midi.* Here at least I might feel I was myself a Catholic. For the doctrine is essentially a Catholic one, is it not?

Falling in love has finished the work, and has completely enlightened me as to this imperative need in myself. Before it happened I believed a certain subtle arrangement of my life was possible, studious solitude, a slow and deliberate enjoyment of my own intelligence. But even then my heart revolted at what my reason presented as a sovereign good. In a word, I may have *thought* it the higher counsel; but I *felt* that it was false and delusive. I have understood since how impossibly insufficient for me it always was. For me, self-satisfaction will never come save through self-consummation. There is no question of constraint in the case. My life simply passes most naturally in spending my substance physical and spiritual.

I imagine I shall not have time to write to you again before your arrival in Europe, which I look forward to, yet dread terribly. You will cast an indulgent eye on my emotion, will you not? I would like a line from you telling me exactly when you are to be expected and where I shall be able to see you.

Assuring you, dear great friend, of my respectful and profound affection,

J. Rivière

To Jacques Rivière
28TH APRIL, 1909

My dear friend,

I am still quite uncertain when I shall return to France. It will certainly not be before the autumn.

The offer from the Théatre d'Art gave me the idea of re-reading *la Jeune Fille Violaine*, at which I had not even glanced since I corrected the final proofs. Alas, what a blow to vanity! These old things leave the impression of so many threadbare garments lying at the bottom of an old trunk, and still vaguely retaining the contours of the body they once clad. To think that one loved—that one moved about, in these things! An idea has struck me which will help me to make the piece scenic. It will mean re-casting the character of Pierre de Craon, and leaving out the architectural stuff at the end.

What a fluid medium writers like ourselves work in! No wonder that the rules of prosody are invoked to give it, at least from the outside, an appearance of artificial rigidity.

What I find so vapid in all the wise writers of antiquity, and what once rendered certain stretches of the *Selectae* absolutely intolerable to me, is their theory of moderation in the feelings and passions. The ideal of wisdom among the Greeks and their followers, Epictetus, for example, is an uneventful, mediocre life. There is nothing instinctive nor fundamentally human in this ideal. For a long time it prevented me from understanding the Aristotelian theory of ρεσον, on which all moral theology is founded. Latterly I have found several pages full of merit and wit on this subject by a fantastic English writer (G. K. Chesterton: *Orthodoxy*). He shows that Christian doctrine differs from all others, because it places wisdom, not in a certain mediocre neutrality, but in apparently contradictory sentiments, pushed to their utmost degree of intensity. (Joy and penance, pride and humility, love and renunciation, etc.) Man is as though stretched out upon a cross, and undergoes simultaneously tension and extension in every sense of the words. It is an application in the moral domain of a theory of "perpendicular truths" that I seem to remember having once advanced. *Quantum potes, tantum aude.* This is the great device of Christian art and civilization. It is this which once made Europe something more than a stupid Empire of the average.

Affectionately,

P. Claudel

To Jacques Rivière

VILLENEUVE-SUR-FÈRE (AISNE), 14TH SEPTEMBER, 1909

Heartfelt wishes, my dear Rivière, for your happiness and for that of your bride, whom I can imagine so young and so gracious, and also for the family that you are founding. God has led you to happiness by the shortest route there is. You see now that none who seek Him are left without some reward from His munificence.

I am resting here with my wife and children after a terrible journey. I shall not be definitely at Paris till November. Then I count upon the pleasure of seeing you and speaking with you.

I am writing this in a barn where I have taken refuge to escape from the turmoil of a little house full of callers. Here, every morning, the hens and I are company for one another. They brood over their eggs—I over my manuscript.

With sincerest regards to Madame Rivière.

Believe me affectionately yours,

P. Claudel

To Jacques Rivière

HOSTEL VIRIEU-LA-GRANDE, 12TH OCTOBER, 1909

My dear friend,

You may consider the affair as settled. I have spoken to our friend Abbè M——, proctor of the Collège Stanislas. All he insists upon now is a few questions on philosophy. You may call upon him at any time.

I am staying in the most beautiful country conceivable, still aflame with the glorious tints of autumn. God is giving me a very happy life and treats me like a spoiled child (sometimes I fancy with just a little disdain).

My regards to Madame Rivière and to your brother-in-law.

P. Claudel

I have just had a visit from young Henrion, who is on his way to Rome.

To Jacques Rivière

7 RUE DE LA TRÈMOILLE, 10TH NOVEMBER, 1909

My dear Rivière,

I would like to find some way of having a little more friendly talk with you than we have found possible up to now. I shall be at the eight o'clock mass tomorrow at Notre Dame. We can take a short walk afterwards. If I don't see you, I shall understand you could not come. I shall be leaving Paris soon. As ever.

P. Claudel

To Paul Claudel

PARIS, SUNDAY, 30TH JANUARY, 1910

My dear great friend,

I am writing to you from the heart of the flood. Our street is the only one on the quarter which has been spared. All around us people are getting about in boats. You have no idea of the extraordinary sights we have witnessed during these last few days. They have made such an impression on me that I may try to do something with them later on.

I did not write you sooner because I have been absolutely absorbed by new endeavors of every sort. I do not feel I have the strength to plunge into the deadening work of a fellowship: it would mean deterioration. I have no talent whatever for teaching. So, with all its horrors, I have made up my mind to the miserable career of a writer. I feel that my duty lies here. I am not proud of the profession. But, since I am called to it there is nothing to do but accept it. At least it is no more humiliating than any other. I know what I shall have to do, and already am no stranger to some of its tasks. But I am not afraid. The really humiliating thing is to hang back.

Besides, a life that demands everything, more even than I can give, is the life I must have. Happiness is impossible for me unless I am absorbed and torn in every direction by incessant controversy. I dare not be my own man—it is then that despair overtakes me and I become really wicked. To be worth anything I need to succumb again and again. Oh, I know well the new life will be merciless—that embracing it means sacrificing peace, independence and solitude. It is for this very reason I choose it.

Please do not see in this sudden change of plans a sign of weakness or hesitancy. I have acquired the habit of seeing in every event a finger-post showing me the road I am to follow. The reason I prepared for my fellowship so deliberately, was to be sure that if I failed, I should not be justified in going on hoping. It would be my last chance this year. Why should I persist uselessly, and put off writing what I felt driven to write? Courage is one thing and obstinacy is another.

I find that I am excusing myself to you as if I looked for reproaches. This is because I know you considered me predestined for a professorship. But in my heart I do not believe God ever meant it to be my vocation. What I say is not written to convince you. I myself had always seen in the teaching profession a mere means of earning a good living, and not any special mission. It is far better that I abandon it.

* * * * *

Your coming home has caused me great distress of spirit. Many of the excuses I gave you for my lack of belief have been demolished by our talks together. What has upset me more than anything else, is the new fashion in which I shall henceforth have to regard Catholicism. Instead of considering it as a lancet that probes my wounds, a humiliation to perfect my humility, a desperate remedy that works by destroying all my confidence in things of earth, you teach it to me as a balance to be attained, a measure to follow, an attitude exact as the rules of good health. Yet, suppose I have no desire for health? Suppose I am too sick and too much in love with my malady to desire a cure? So long as I could look forward to an annihilation of my whole being, to something in which I could sink, and from whose depths, suddenly, a broad daylight would dawn upon me, I was full of anxious expectancy. But now you tell me that I must work out my own salvation, that I must employ my intelligence to weave the tissue of truth thread by thread, that I alone can attain the things that are to my peace. Where am I to find hope—the will even, to save myself thus? I am too deeply stricken by now to wish for a cure. Let an end be made of me! To this I can resign myself, but to nothing else.

Forgive me, my best of friends! I am conscious myself that what I say is an evil excuse, an exhalation from my own lethargy. And yet, I pray; I go to mass! You must not be too hard on me. For *this is the truth*: I am suffering from not feeling my thirst as acute as it was a few months ago. I am in despair I know what my goal must be. And how shall I ever reach it, if the desire for it dies down in me?

With my most profound and respectful friendship.

J. Rivière

To Jacques Rivière

PRAGUE, CANDLEMAS DAY

My dear friend,

You were right in foreseeing that your decision to give up teaching would distress me deeply. There is no worse profession in the world than that of a writer who has to live by his pen. And here are you, constrained henceforth to produce with one eye upon a patron, the public—to give him, not what you love, but what he likes, and God knows how elevated and refined his taste has always been! Say what you like—rather than lead the life of a Monsieur X, I would cobble shoes. I always think of tragic figures like Villiers de l'Isle Adam, or Verlaine, with the relics of their talent clinging to them, like the fur on a moth-eaten coat. It is not an honorable thing to live on one's soul and to peddle it to strangers. The contempt the world has always had for actors and artists is a quite legitimate one.

And you are a married man!

Your reasons don't convince me. They are those of a woman, who wants to misconduct herself and who is attracted by the prospect of an adventurous and exciting life. Duty, virtue, talent, science, everything noble and of good repute, suddenly appear monotonous and boresome. Time, patience, and peace of mind are all needed to compose anything worth while. I never seen anything except trash come out of a whirl. You are very ready to find providential indications. If there is one that seems to me more marked than another in your case, it is the one that has led you to the professorate. You are perfectly capable of gaining your fellowship if you want to, even if you have to wait, one, two or three years. Anything is better than the gutter.

You have one great fault. It is the way you exaggerate your weakness, your incapacity for any dull, prolonged task. You always want to prove that life is in the wrong. Life is life. But you stand at a point where an excess of despondency or a hasty decision may have results for you that I shudder to contemplate. I repeat to you with all the energy of which I am capable, and with the full memory of certain terrible examples in my mind's eye: there is no worse trade than literature!

As a professor, you have four or five hours a day in class, and two or three months' vacation every year. This is not so very terrible. The life you find so tempting will teach you what real drudgery is. This is no time for you to be making literature of your life. I know I am speaking harshly to you. But I do not mind your hating me so long as you listen to reason. You have wonderful gifts—a combination of some of the finest qualities. But you spoil everything by your morbid craving to feel yourself a victim and an exile. This *Sojourn in Hell* must come to an end. Remember the phrase with which it ends and which I have so often recited to myself: "No more tears! Consider only what we have won! The morning dawns, when, armed with patient ardor, we shall enter into resplendent cities!"

Poor child! In all affection, I extend to you the hand of—

P. Claudel

To Paul Claudel

TUESDAY, 15TH FEBRUARY, 1910

Dear and great friend,

My reply has been delayed by influenza. It must begin by congratulations, as yesterday we heard that you were again a father. My wife begs me to let you know that she joins in my wishes for your happiness.

Your letter affected me very deeply. I was hardly prepared for your violent objections to something I looked upon as settled. But I thank you for having made them. Be sure of this—I shall never think the worse of you for scolding me. You have made me ponder. And before anything else I want to let you know where I feel you are right.

It is quite true that I give up easily, that I like to think of myself as a wounded and disinherited creature, that I am cowardly at times; or, rather, it is true that I accept suffering a little too readily rather than look it full in the face—and then afterwards blame myself because I did not.

It is true that I have no taste for irksome tasks, for looking far ahead, for beginning in a small way and counting my gains up day by day. I plunged into the work for my fellowship exam in a sort of fury that kept me up till the end. I shall never have the same energy again.

It is true that it is better not to have to earn one's bread through selling one's soul—to have security and liberty. It is no less true that peace of mind is an indispensable thing.

But I am not like yourself, a man full of health and strength. I have not the constitution which permits a man to settle himself once for all in a certain way of life and to accomplish things one after another. I have not time to wait *three years* for a fellowship. Even if I liked tiresome tasks, even if I had the moral courage to become a student again, I could not compromise what I feel I have to do by any such delay.

And, then, remember that even if I had a hundred years of life before me, I have not now—at this moment—the strength to study philosophy. My brain is feeble and the slightest work tires it. As soon as I concentrate violently (and for me philosophy always entails a tremendous expenditure of mental energy) I lose all faculty for lucidity. Last year I had a headache that lasted two months and a half. I was so dazed that I could think of nothing. I was always asking myself how much of that horrible confusion I had suffered would remain in my brain. I had nightmares throughout which I was seeking interminably to reconcile the various absurdities of Hume's philosophy.

Naturally, I would like to attain peace, calm, silence. But I have known for a long time that, in this world anyhow, they are not for me. They are things that people talk about, and never get. I am not so simple-minded as to believe that a fellowship would procure them for me. I made up my mind long ago that, since trouble, anxiety and insecurity were the only boons life was going to bestow upon me, I had best make up my mind to acquire a love for them.

This is not saying that I like disorder. I hate it. And if I really had to choose between a life of routine and "the gutter" I would not hesitate a moment. But I do not believe there is any such alternative. I believe I can gain an honest and sufficient livelihood by my pen. I have no desire to be another Villiers or Verlaine, and my work is not going to resemble theirs in any way. Remember that I am, primarily, a critic, and that it is far easier for a critic to say loyally what he thinks than for a poet to write pure verse. I can surely make a living, and yet keep my independence, if I set myself to understand and to expound without any idea of flattering the public. I don't mean to say that I am going to do nothing but criticism, nor that I want to make it the major part of my work. But we are speaking from the practical point of view. And I merely claim that in my capacity as a critic I have an asset that is not to be despised. Consider also that, as professor in the provinces, I would be missing the matter on which to exercise this faculty.

Don't imagine that I take my literary vocation tragically or think that everything is to be sacrificed to art. I know that each thing has its own value. But great Heavens! Do you reproach me for wanting to do what is prescribed me—and for wanting to do it just as soon as possible? I have my own mission in life. And I assure you that it is not teaching. I should be a poor professor, while I may yet be a good writer. Of that, at least, I am sure, and nothing can convince me otherwise. It is not vanity that tells me this.

I would add that the arguments I advanced in my letter are not so contemptible as they seem to you. I did not invent them for the occasion. They correspond to profound beliefs which I will try to explain for you—and which make up my moral character.

You see that my decision, rash as it may be, has more than one reason behind it. I did not make it through weakness. Nevertheless, you have shaken me a little. Perhaps I shall try my fate again. I will make a hasty preparation, necessarily incomplete, and will try to deceive my examiners upon the extent of my knowledge (I know nothing of philosophy). I may succeed, as others have done. Don't tell me it is dishonest. It is the only means I have at the present moment. I have not opened one book of the syllabus and I have my twenty-eight days[†] to do in March.

Best of friends, I must thank you again. How great a support to me are your affection and advice. All the more so, perhaps, because they are so terribly uncompromising.

Assuring you of my respectful friendship and of the joy your new happiness gives me.

Jacques Rivière

† Of military duty, as a member of the reserve.

To Jacques Rivière

PRAGUE, 17TH FEBRUARY, 1910

My dear boy,

First of all, forgive me the way I wrote to you a few weeks ago. I had no right to take such a tone. My letter was no sooner in the mail than I was ashamed of it. That does not mean I promise not to begin again. You must treat me like one of those cross-grained old vixens whose scoldings no one takes seriously.

Even while I excuse myself for the inadmissible tone of my good advice, I cannot pretend I think it bad. I have more experience than you. You will never be an X——or a Y——. They are the winners in this horrible existence. One is forced to admit it. But how many have been sucked in and have disappeared.

Poor child!—just make this simple calculation. From the moment you want to make money by your pen, you have to consider the tastes of your *clientèle.* Do you believe that, for the critical articles you will write, one exists sufficiently large to assure you the regular and independent existence which it is your duty, as the head of a family, to try to secure? If you have tremendously good luck, you will be taken on some big journal where you will be forced to write, not what suits you, but what suits the two masters whose yoke you have chosen: I mean the *owner* and the *subscriber.*

This is not meant to turn you away from literary criticism, for which you feel a legitimate vocation, and for which you have gifts of the very first order. But don't confuse a luxury with a livelihood. If an insurmountable disgust repels you from teaching, at least, I beg of you, try to procure yourself some means of earning your bread which will permit you to exercise your talents safely in the field you contemplate. Be an employé, be an overseer in one of the municipal departments like Philippe! But procure yourself some resources which will save you from the mercies of our literary slave-drivers. Your contributions will always find easier acceptance if it is known you don't depend on them for a livelihood.

Poor boy! God keep and guard you! It is hard to watch a young man entering upon this awful road of the arts, and to remain unmoved.

Thank you for your kind wishes. We had a terrible house-moving, in mid-winter, into an apartment house full of painters, with an infant born before time, and my wife, who had to be carried on a litter. However, everything turned out well!

And they tell me that in Paris the rain is still falling!

Kindest regards to Madame Rivière. Affectionately,

P. Claudel

The last number of the *N.R.F.*† on Philippe is superb!

† *Nouvelle Revue Française.*

To Jacques Rivière
PRAGUE, 23RD FEBRUARY, 1910

My dear friend,

Now you know the worst. I have opened my heart to you. I have said what my great regard for you and the sad experiences that I have had urged me to: some fine day you may remember it all and say, "Well, Claudel was a good fellow; he gave me sound advice." But advice never does much good, and there is much truth in the proverb that "advisers are not payers." God keep you, dear friend, in the new life to which my unchangeable affection accompanies you.

As for the article on me you have been asked for, do whatever you think right, dear Rivière, and entitle it as you please. Everyone, by now, alas, knows that I am a host for the literary virus. All I would ask of you is not to speak about my philosophical or religious opinions.

While unpacking, I came across *Orthodoxy* by Chesterton. I am translating the opening chapter for the *N.R.F.*, that is, if they want it. It is rather long, and no doubt would have to appear in two sections.

My wife thanks you for your message. Please remember me to yours. With kind regards to Gide.

Sincerely,

P. Claudel

To Paul Claudel

CENON, NEAR BORDEAUX, 3RD APRIL, 1910

Dear and great friend,

I have let a long time elapse since your last letter. One of the terrible drawbacks of this life (I knew it in advance) is that it takes up every spare moment and deprives one of any chance to concentrate. Perhaps this, too, is a blessing in disguise....

I want to relieve your anxiety by telling you that, thanks to you, I shall possibly find a steady job at Paris. Abbé M——, quite of his own accord, has offered me one of the chairs of philosophy at the Collège Stanislas for next year. Nothing is decided definitely yet, but I have every reason to hope. I will not conceal from you that one of the conditions he makes is that I continue preparing for my fellowship. But once things are settled and I have something like regular hours, perhaps I shall be able to manage this too.

Meantime (but this is a secret between Gide and myself) the *N.R.F.* has offered me a small standing salary for regular contributions, which will be a great help. I am also writing articles in *Art et Décoration*: at least, I have written and been paid for one, which will be followed, I hope, by others.

I have not yet been able to set about my monograph: *Paul Claudel*, for the *Paris-Journal*. I feel a little tired after my work for the April number of the *N.R.F.*, and was obliged to go to the country to rest. The moment I get back to Paris I will start upon you.

I have also had an offer to become editor of a small review, *l'Art Libre*, which proposes to consecrate its July number to your work. It wants me to write an article on one of its phases. I have accepted and will no doubt speak of the *Hymns* and of the *Odes*, if they have appeared by then. But they want you to send them something too, if only a page. And I am charged to forward this request. I have to admit I know nothing of the review. But its program seems to deserve encouragement.

I am here surrounded by the miraculous whiteness of fruit trees in blossom. For a week we have had such marvelous weather that one has the sensation of being afloat upon some tranquil and illimitable ocean. But fine weather is as unsupportable to me as tranquillity. It drowns my soul in a suffocating sweetness. It leaves me to myself: and this is the thing of which I am most afraid. Don't imagine, on this account, that I am hardening into indifference. On the contrary, I have learned to pray with something like violence.

Go on writing me. I will answer you, I promise it, without so long a delay again. You will always do me a world of good. From now on, every time I get one of your letters, I shall say to myself: What a good fellow Claudel is, and how happy I am to have met him!

I beg you to present my respects to Mme. Claudel and to believe me very profoundly and humbly your friend,

Jacques Rivière

To Jacques Rivière

PRAGUE, 7TH APRIL, 1910

My dear friend,

Your letter filled me with pleasure. You tell me that you have acquired a taste for prayer and persevere in it. If you know how to look around you, you will already perceive its fruit. *De Oratione tua fiet tibi.*† You used to ask me for some indication from Providence. Could there be one clearer than this sudden and unhoped offer from the Collège Stanislas, which will assure you consideration and security in the future?

The fact that it was made you proves to me also that you do yourself an injustice as to your own qualities. Abbé M——is a very shrewd and practical man. You may be confident that he would never have offered you this position if he had not been sure you were qualified to fill it. At Stanislas you will be in good and honorable company, and will find the tranquillity which, whatever you may think about it, is absolutely necessary for the development of our higher faculties. Your intercourse with profound thinkers and the familiarity with lofty speculation which will be yours as a professor cannot but be profitable. I would add that if you desire a firm friend and an excellent adviser, you will find one in Abbé M——. He has a clear and vigorous mind and, at the same time, the best of hearts, and you can rely upon his judgment.

† According to your prayer be it done unto you.

You tell me you have made great progress. I know it, I can see it, and I thank God for it. All I am sorry for is that you came upon so poor a guide in me. I am violent and too easily carried away. You should have found someone gentler and with more patience. But the perfect friend will never be found in this world. It is He of Whom the gospels tell us in this beautiful week on the threshold of Pentecost. "*Beatae aures quae venas divini susurri suscipiunt!*" Would that one day you might partake with us this Easter banquet which we have just left. "*Convivium pinguium, convivium vindemiae pinguium medullatorum, vindemiae defoecatae*" (Isaiah). Pardon me for talking Latin to you like a curé, but these old texts are so magnificent. (It is by the same Isaiah that the peace of churches set in the midst of great cities is so well described: "*Spes a turbine, umbraculum ab aestu.*")

With my respects to Madame Rivière.

Affectionately yours,

P. Claudel

To Paul Claudel

PARIS, 5TH JUNE, 1910

My dear and great friend,

Another letter from you that I have left two months without answering. You must forgive me. I have been passing through a period of great mental stress and am not yet quite out of the wood.

* * * * *

I must tell you first how kind Abbé M—— has been and what good services he has rendered me. He got me a lot of lessons, indeed I have so many pupils at the moment that I hardly know how to grapple with them, and this is one of the reasons for my fatigue.

Nothing is settled yet for next year. Probably I shall only have a few hours a week to begin with. But that is just what I want. Teaching comes very hard to me and I don't want it to consume too much of my energy.

Abbé M——is just the man you described. There is something exquisite in his cordiality.

My miserable head is still preventing me writing that article upon you for *Paris-Journal.* I have begun it three times and had to give it up. For one thing, it is a very difficult and delicate subject. I am a bad hand at generalities. I need some precise matter that calls for examination. How can one speak of your work in two columns? And if I choose one phase of it only, I risk giving an idea of it that is false because it is partial. Still, I have by no means given up the idea. I am merely waiting till a little strength and good spirits come back to me.

At this moment I am working hard upon your *Odes* and your *Hymns* for *l'Art Libre.* That is why I don't care to speak to you just now about the *Magnificat*, which stirs me so deeply. In my article I am going to say something about my admiration for this newest of the *Odes*, and to explain the very special point of view from which I admire it. Do you mind my saying that I am less directly touched by your lyric poetry than by your plays? Not that I find it less fine, but it seems to have less to say to me. It is when I read the *Magnificat* that I realize how very far still I am from being a Christian, at least such a Christian as yourself. How impossible of realization such a joy seems! How many sorrows that I find too profitable to let go of! My great fault lies here. I know it. I know that no one has the right to grow fond of something that is doing him harm. But where am I to find the strength to break away?

Do you really and truly believe that there are men, apart from yourself, who can reach this total renunciation of every weakness? I ask you this question in all honesty, and through desire for information. Try for a moment to imagine a soul different from your own. Do you believe that it can, being what it is, shake off its miseries and grievances? To hear you say: "Yes," would be an immense help to me. But do not say so unless you feel it from the very bottom of your heart.

Assuring you of my immense respect and affection,

J. Rivière

To Paul Claudel

PARIS, 27TH JULY, 1910

Dear great friend,

I am just back from Normandy where I have spent three delightful weeks with Gide, and am off to the Cher for a month. Thence I will go to Bordeaux for my twenty-eight days. In October I enter Stanislas as professor of philosophy (on probation) in the classes that are taking up the St. Cyr and Agricultural College examinations. Thanks to Abbé M——I have arranged with the director to draw 1,500 or 1,650 francs a year for four and a half hours a week and one extra hour every fortnight. With a few lessons and examinations I believe I shall be well enough off. I am very deeply indebted to you for having helped me into the college by your recommendation.

What decided the director to take me on the teaching staff was that of my ten pupils, seven passed, two with honors. Among the three that failed one may be admitted later.

The issue of *l'Art Libre* devoted to you will shortly appear. Please forgive my own article, which I did not have the time to compose as I should.

I leave in a few minutes and have just the time to assure you of my profound and respectful affection.

Jacques Rivière

To Jacques Rivière

PRAGUE, 25TH AUGUST, 1910

My dear friend,

The mailman has just brought me the number of *l'Art Libre*, containing your fine study on my poetry. I notice that, since your long article in *l'Occident*, I am being spoken of in a different and much more intelligent fashion. In this review, too, it is quite evident how you have influenced your two neighbors. You also help me to understand certain passages in your letters that puzzled me a little at the time. What I like most in your work is that there is neither flattery nor blame, but the two eyes of an understanding man. How much this means to an artist! But does my verse really seem so inhuman and cruel to you? I had a notion that I was much tenderer and more compassionate. The fault must lie in my long years of absolute loneliness.

Everything you say about my method of composition is very good indeed. All the paragraph beginning: "A secret thought..."(p. 365) and what follows are especially well observed and expressed. I am not a man who thinks consecutively and piecemeal. Each thought is a complete entity—is never developed without the consonance or dissonance of other thought-entities making itself apparent. Naturally, certain parts emerge above the others. But they are all inherent to an *ensemble*, which protests if I attempt to violate its unity. Everything takes its start from a sort of interior rumbling, amid which, more or less defined, certain detached gleams begin to appear, the poem being still submerged.

By now I imagine you will have received the *Odes.* I see that you are already quite prepared to understand the three which you do not know yet and which are the most difficult.

Tell me some news of yourself. I hope the stay at Cuverville has done you good. I am delighted at your nomination to Stanislas. It means an assured future under the most honorable conditions.

With respects to Madame Rivière.

Yours sincerely,

P. Claudel

To Paul Claudel

THURSDAY, 1ST DECEMBER, 1910

Dear friend,

It is only during the last few days that I found time to read the *Odes*, and to blame myself for having thanked you so poorly for such a splendid present. Not only in its poetic content but in the beauty of its type, it is a monumental affair. When I read you I can hardly keep myself from showing my appreciation by a sort of nervous laugh that comes from intense satisfaction. No man was ever a poet to such a monstrous degree as yourself.

I shall have to read the *Five Odes* over and over before I dare to say that I own them. Just now I feel particularly fond of the first two and the fifth. This is not saying that the two others are not fine. I regret very much that I had not read the entire book before writing my article. I could have been more explicit in certain parts of it, and have made use of more striking quotations.

The idea occurred to me during these last few days of publishing the two articles I wrote on you in book-form. For the moment I have not found a publisher but have not tried very hard yet. I presume that you would have no objection.

Please forgive me, also, for having used certain ideas that I got from you in an article on Baudelaire that I have just sent to the *N.R.F.* I am not much in love with it. I wrote it too quickly and under unfavorable "cerebral" conditions. I will revise it from end to end before including it in a volume of criticism. In the second half, it seems to me I have constructed a sort of "*Baudelaire malgré lui.*" I have stressed certain ideas which were secret and latent in him, and have brought them to the foreground, rather with the air of believing them exclusive qualities in his thought. You will see what I mean later.—What consoles me is that possibly the presence of these ideas in Baudelaire deserve to be exaggerated, because they are the ones everybody else has turned a blind eye to. Even if I seem to err, my exaggerations themselves should serve the cause of Baudelaire. At least, I hope so.

Before writing this article, I re-read and learnt by heart all of the *Fleurs du mal.* There is no greater French poet than Baudelaire!

Will you allow me to say that I hardly consider you a *French* poet. Your work has no precursor in our literary past. You fall among us from the skies, violent, formidable and unlooked-for. That is why, just now, in all deliberation, I used the word "monstrous." To find your predecessor, we would have to go back to the Greeks. Even Shakespeare, even Dante, do not foreshadow you. You are not of their succession, but, simply, Greek and biblical. The only thing by which you betray your *Frenchness* is the formidable aptness of your phraseology: it is, after all, our language you speak, and with a power of precision that we hardly suspected—challenging words, time and again, to show forth their origin and their history—to justify their meaning. Yet that very habit of what might be called violent aptness, is the habit of a man who tames a language by his genius, rather than of one who submits to it and follows its fashions.

Forgive me, dear friend, for vivisecting you this way and calling the result a letter. I can only plead that certain ideas came into my head as I read you and that to repeat them is one way of thinking of you. I ask your indulgence in case it displeases you.

I have not yet read *l'Otage.*

Write me when you have a little time to spare. Everything you say does me good. Certain phrases of yours will never get out of my head.

Assuring you of my deep and respectful friendship,

Yours affectionately,

Jacques Rivière

To Jacques Rivière

PRAGUE, 10TH DECEMBER, 1910

My dear friend,

You would be an ungrateful fellow if you did not like the *Odes.* You must have found in them not a few of the ideas and preoccupations which filled the long letters I was writing to you at the time, and which I took a great deal of pains over—without result, alas, bad boy that you are! What is really an innovation in these poems is that they are authentic symphonies, not developed consecutively after the literary manner, but by interweaving and analysing different themes just as in orchestration.

No, I do not care greatly for your article on Baudelaire. You wrote it too hurriedly, and I do not find in it the same pungency and depth as when you wrote on me for the *l'Art Libre,* or as the excellent note upon André Lhote that I find in the same number. Its chief fault is a lack of design and composition. Every artist who is born comes into the world to say just one little thing. To find that one little thing and to group all the rest around it is the critic's business. You did well to re-read the *Fleurs du mal.* But you should also have read *le Coeur mis à nu,* which is the real key to Baudelaire (I wonder do you know of this astonishing fragmental novel?) and some passages from *Curiosités Esthétiques.* These last would have given you Baudelaire's idea for a vast compendium of modern poetry à la Balzac, of which whatever he accomplished was only a partial realization. The quotation you give from me about the journalistic style has been better developed by Gide, who speaks of the masterly negligence of these verses, where the man of every day, "my fellow-creature and my brother," is never concealed beneath a bookish or artificial personality.

* * * * *

How are you getting on with your duties at Stanislas? Are all your misgivings at an end?

Affectionately,

P. Claudel

To Paul Claudel

PARIS, 1ST JUNE, 1911

Dear friend,

I have not written you for a long time. But you have been silent too. This made it all the pleasanter to receive your new *Tête d'Or.* Thank you infinitely for your present. You know what a passionate and limitless admiration I have for your early books. I have found more good in them than in any other contemporary author whatsoever. For me they have meant a positive metaphysical revelation. Nothing ever so stirred me to the depths of my being as verses like these:

Et les âmes nouvellement nées le long des murs et des bois,
Poussant comme les petits oiseaux tout nus de faibles cris,
Refuient guidées par les météores vers les régions de l'obscurité.

You know I would not tell you these things if they were not true. I sometimes blame myself for not having insisted sufficiently, in my study of you, on a certain element in your plays that is terrifying in its depth. I mean something that surpasses immediate reality and rings *supernaturally* true.

I had been meaning, for some time, to write you and tell you a very great and very personal piece of news. I am going to become a father. In September. You will understand the impatience and anxiety with which I look forward to that month.

Just at the moment I am working at a rather long article on Gide, which is to be published, I hope soon, in *la Grande Révue.* When that is done I shall start collecting my critical essays for publication in book form. This will appear, I think, some time in October.

I would like to be quite sure, that my vague criticisms on *l'Otage*, to which, in any case, I do not attach great value, have not displeased you. I shall re-read the book in the edition which the *N.R.F.* are getting out, and have no doubt I shall take immense pleasure in it. What I said really came from a regret at something I seemed to see you abandoning. I have taken such delight in your verse that I could not help grieving a little at this sudden turn to austerity and severity. Now I see things differently. I am convinced that you are right. You are one of those souls who are always right.

A letter from you (I ask but a word) would give me so much pleasure and do me so much good! Please convey my respects to Madame Claudel and believe me deeply, persistently, inveterately—and unworthily—your friend,

J. Rivière

To Jacques Rivière

PRAGUE, 5TH JUNE, 1911

My dear Rivière,

How foolish of you to think that your remarks upon *l'Otage* would displease me! On the contrary, they interest me very much. You can never be too sincere with me. Nothing is so priceless for an author as a frank impression, especially when it comes from an intelligence as delicate as yours, and which tells him just *where* and *how* his work has reacted. I beg that you will always feel absolutely free where mine is concerned. Besides, every one of my books is in the nature of an investigation. My theories are so many temporary scaffoldings which disappear as soon as the building is finished. I have never looked upon my art as an end in itself; rather as a means, multiple and diverse, of understanding through renewed acts of creation. *L'Annonce faite à Marie*, which I am just finishing, will probably please you more than *l'Otage*. Nevertheless the results achieved by the very painful studies that the latter play entailed, will not be lost. It is really not worth while repeating the same book indefinitely. Once an idea has been thoroughly exploited, a writer should try to pass on to fresh territory.

I am deeply moved by the news you send me. May God and Our Holy Mother protect the dear young wife! The women of my own family who are in this condition send to an old convent in Brittany for a blessed ribbon, and there have never been any accidents with us. I can give you the address. You are about to discover that there is nothing better in the world than to be a father and to hold one of these precious little beings in one's arms.

I leave for France on Thursday. Between the 12th and 22nd, I shall spend a few days at Paris and Villeneuve. I hope that we shall meet.

With kind regards to Madame Rivière,

Yours affectionately,

P. Claudel

To Jacques Rivière

PARIS, 21ST JUNE, 1911

Dear friend,

I shall be back in Paris, from Saturday to Tuesday, after a short stay at Villeneuve. Could we meet Monday, at whatever hour suits you best?

Sincerely,

P. Claudel

To Paul Claudel
PARIS, 26TH JULY, 1911

Dear friend,

Forgive me for not having given you news of *l'Annonce faite* à *Marie.* Only the muddle-headedness which is the result of cramming for my examination could have prevented me telling you what I had done with the MSS and how reading it overwhelmed me.

On the second point I feel too tired now to enter. I will merely say that, compared with *la Jeune fille Violaine*, there is a tragic depth of writing that makes it an absolute portent. The *Prologue* seems to me the finest thing you have ever written. I cried without ceasing from end to end of it.

I cannot write you as long a letter as I would like on account of my examination. I hope to hear soon that I am plucked. Then I shall be free again.

Don't forget the address of the ribbon. My wife is as well as can be expected. But we are having stifling weather which tires her a little.

Thank you very much for sending me *la Ville.* At last I have the first version in something besides a shabby typewritten copy.

Affectionately and faithfully yours,

Jacques Rivière

P.S. Could you tell me just where in the Bible (Old or New Testament) I can find an explanation of the phrase: "Bethlehem: the House of Bread"?

To Jacques Rivière
PRAGUE, 26TH JULY, 1911

Dear friend,

Here at last is the address for the ribbon: Write to M. le curé at Quintin (Cotes du Nord). I trust that this little act of simple confidence in the Blessed Virgin by Madame Rivière will be rewarded, as it has never failed to be with us.

* * * * *

Wishing you all luck in your examination.

Affectionately,

P. Claudel

Have you read the magnificent article by Péguy in the *Bulletin des professeurs catholiques de l'Université* declaring himself definitely a Catholic?

To Jacques Rivière
PRAGUE, 28TH JULY, 1911

My dear friend,

The principal test relative to Bethlehem is that of the prophet Michaiah, quoted by Matthew: *Et tu, Bethlehem, tu es parvulus in millibus Juda: ex te enim mihi egredietur, qui erit dominator in Israel, et egressus ejus ab initio, a diebus aeternis* (Michaiah, Chap. V, v. 7). An astounding text, by the way, resuming as it does, St. John and the Synoptics! The phrase "House of Bread" is the literal translation of the word Beth-Lehem. Ephrata means "the fruitful." The Bible makes no allusion to this rendering but all the Fathers and commentators have noted it.

* * * * *

I hope that you have the ribbon by now. But there is something that is better than all the ribbons in the world, and that is Holy Communion. It is the absolute *right* of God to be with those who are sick or in peril, as you know Madame Rivière must necessarily be, more or less. It is His place, and must not be refused Him. Remember that you are responsible now for a soul and the full significance of such a responsibility. Put your house in order, and the blessing of God will descend upon it naturally. I tell you this as man to man, and from my heart.

From my heart, too, I pity you for having to work in such a temperature, and have just the strength to sign myself.

Sincerely yours,

P. Claudel

To Paul Claudel

2ND AUGUST, 1911

Dear friend,

I have failed for my fellowship. I am convinced, not, perhaps, that I did everything possible to prepare for it, but at least of having deserved to be classed "admissible" if only for the sake of the compositions which a happy chance enabled me to write. I simply do not understand what happened. But between the spirit of the university and mine there is an antagonism so complete and comprehensive that agreement on any point would be impossible. Whether I do violence to myself, as I did two years ago, or allow myself to be a little more natural, as I have been this year, the university is not deceived. It recognizes in me its enemy.

All this sounds like an alibi to explain my failure. I would like to have been listed "admissible," if only to have had it to say, and to make use of in the future.

Anyhow, I have too many other anxieties for this failure to affect me very much. Thank you for the address of the ribbon. We have written, but have had no reply yet.

Certainly, dear friend, everything shall be "in order" at the moment we are awaiting. You have no idea what a long unsuspected road I have traveled since I first knew you. It is a kind of secret process whose extent surprises myself. And be sure that in the ordeal which we are approaching we will ask every help from God. I will not say more now. I should hate to be classed with those who promise everything and perform nothing. I am slow to move, and crises never get me anywhere. But something is happening, none the less.

* * * * *

Thank you for what you tell me about Bethlehem.

The heat has been prostrating everyone for a fortnight, but it is a little cooler now. I am very slow getting back to work and it seems to me that everything has been piling up for me. As soon as my volume of criticisms is finished, I shall concentrate on my novel.

Write me from time to time. Your letters always do me so much good.

Affectionately yours,

Jacques Rivière

Yes, I read the article by Péguy, with what emotion you can imagine. It is when we see a faith as firm as his and yours expressing itself openly that we realize the distance we have traveled since the nineteenth century.

My article on Gide, slightly cut, will appear in the *Grande Revue* for September.

To Jacques Rivière

PRAGUE, 10TH AUGUST, 1911

My dear friend,

You are right to take your failure quietly and to be satisfied with having done your best. My own opinion is that in these matters it is largely a question of a man's connexion: he has to prove that he is one of the brotherhood. I hope your ill-success will not injure you at Stanislas.

The news you send me gives me much pleasure. Just a little more courage, and then—to horse! You are worthy to be one of us and to ride knee to knee with us, the champions of these strange latter days.

To Jacques Rivière
FRANKFORT-ON-MAIN, 11TH OCTOBER, 1911

Dear friend,

I have heard nothing from you for a long time, but a number of the *N.R.F.* which I have just received shows me that you are still thinking of me. What a genius for patient and discerning insight you possess! You are the ideal reader of whom every author dreams when he writes.

I trust that Madame Rivière is now completely recovered. Send me news of her and of your baby girl. How radiant your house must seem to you with the presence of this little angel sent you from heaven.

I spent the whole month of September dashing through Germany in every direction. Here I am now, representative of the French Republic in the capital of international Jewry! Frankfort is really a very pretty town, though, full of trees and flowers.

Affectionately yours,

P. Claudel

To Paul Claudel

PARIS 17TH OCTOBER, 1911

Dear friend,

You are right, I left you a long time without news. But I have been through so much on account of my wife and little daughter, and at the same time, have had so much work to get off my shoulders that I have not found a moment to write to you.

At last, things seem to be clearing up. My wife was *extremely ill* after her operation, and this was followed by an attack of phlebitis. She is still in bed, but we hope that she will be able to get up at the end of the week. She had an admirable nurse at the hospital, a saintly sister who will be our friend as long as we live.

My little daughter has also passed through many dangers. On the 12th of last month we thought we had lost her. We found her in her cradle, already cold, and had much ado to bring her back to life.

* * * * *

I am only recounting these adventures one by one, dear friend, in order that you may be apprised of them. Please do not dream that I am complaining. Not for one moment did I cease to feel infinite thankfulness to God, or a trust, no less infinite, in His mercy. Not for a moment, even when it was most in peril, did my happiness diminish in my own eyes. And you guess rightly in imagining my house now filled with joy.

I wanted to write you and congratulate you on your promotion. I congratulate myself too, since you are likelier to come frequently to Paris from Frankfort than from Prague.

Coventry Patmore's poems are admirable, and, though I am not acquainted with the English text, I feel that your translation of them is admirable too.

Remember that all news coming from you is welcome and believe me,

Very faithfully your friend,

Jacques Rivière

To Jacques Rivière

FRANKFORT ON MAIN, 8TH OCTOBER, 1912

My dear Rivière,

If you see Gallimard, please ask him what he is doing with my *Cantate*. He has had it a month and I have heard nothing from him yet. I leave tomorrow for Paris and shall be there about ten days.—My *Rimbaud* is very fleshless and desiccated. I would have a great deal to add to it today, especially as, thanks to meeting some one who knew him, I can now imagine the Rimbaud of the Red Sea. The "adolescent and amoral aspect" is insufficiently stressed. The same thing applies to the animal side, the terrible "stallion" poet that Rimbaud was at seventeen. But, however badly expressed, the essential of what I wanted to say is there.

* * * * *

The great effort that must have gone to the composition of the *Géorgiques* (successfully, I consider) demands that justice be done the first great poem in our literature—since when? The distich form is not adopted with any sententious end in view, but in order to introduce the impression of proliferation and variety, as in a great meadow. With as skillful a writer as Jammes the occasional *gaucheries* must be considered intentional. Their object is the establishment of values, and the constant ruptures arouse attention.

What is more serious, is the profession of faith of the *N.R.F.* Art first!—art for art's sake! Are we really back there? After all these years of frivolous literature, is that foundered old hobby-horse still in our path? Art for art's sake is not a creative doctrine at all. Something else besides a genteel system of calisthenics is needed to draw anything profound or essential out of a man. The relation of art to morality or of art to religion is an excessively grave, delicate and complicated problem. A few smart sayings will not help to solve it. This much is quite evident—French literature today is dying of libertinage and dilettantism. Beyond anything else it lacks *heart* and *tone.* I imagined the *N.R.F.* intended to dedicate itself to the cause of energy in the domain of art. And here we are, back to the futile dissertations of 1885!

Cordially,

P. Claudel

To Jacques Rivière
PARIS, 12TH OCTOBER, 1912

Dear friend,

You know I shall be very glad to see you. Fix some time on Thursday, at your house, as I am not at my own place in Paris. The best thing would be for you to send me your book so that I would have time to read it and think it over.

What a pity that when it becomes necessary for the *N.R.F.* to adopt a doctrine, it should be that of: Art first!—Art for Art's sake!—in other words that of the *Mercure de France!* (It would be better to say, quite frankly: Art for the satisfaction of the senses.) If Jammes ever said that it was enough to be a Christian to be an artist, he said something not so much extravagant as ridiculous. There is no room here even for discussion. Individually, a man can be at the same time a good Christian and a pitiful artist (the Nazarenes, Louis Racine, etc.). But, socially, it is a different matter. In a society such as ours, that is to say, a society which cares for nothing but material enjoyment, the artist, if he is not in possession of a moral force at least equivalent to the terrible and deadly weight which pulls him down, is doomed either to despair and destruction, or to the production of literary kick-shaws. The examples of such men as Poe, Baudelaire, Rimbaud, Verlaine and many another should be enough to warn us. It is in this sense that truth is the condition of beauty, because truth alone can isolate beauty from its deleterious *milieu* and permit it the use of the faculties grace has accorded it.

Ask any artist today who does not believe in God—who does not work solely for the glory of God, *for whom does he work*? For himself? If so, he is in a vicious circle. Oneself is the means, but cannot be the end. For others, then? For their pleasure? For their amusement?

Religion does not create new faculties in us. But it does permit us the use of those we have.

The whole question is extremely difficult and complex. Jammes shows us the sole salvation possible, though perhaps his exposition is inadequate. The *N.R.F.* would lead us back to the horrible old road, strewn with the martyrdoms of so many great artists. Art first! The *means* first!

I thought the review had been founded mainly to free us from that kind of art—an "art" which we know only too well.

Do you believe for a moment that Shakespeare, or Dostoievsky, or Rubens, or Titian, or Wagner, did their work *for art's sake*? No! They did it to free themselves as best they might from their burden, to deliver themselves of a great incubus of living matter, *opus non factum*. And certainly not to color a cold, artificial design by borrowings from reality.

Sincerely yours,

P. Claudel

To Jacques Rivière

FRANKFORT-ON-MAIN, 7TH NOVEMBER, 1912

Dear friend,

You can guess with what interest I took up the first portion of your *Essay on Faith.* I will have more to say when I have seen the whole of it. But I am quite enchanted by what I have already read. I do not say that plenty of objections might not be made to you on theological or philosophical grounds. For instance, you do not seem to me to distinguish sufficiently between faith and credulity. You have all the air of saying that, in your eyes, the nature of what one believes is a matter of indifference—and that, on the contrary, the more absurd the things credited the robuster faith will be. Hence, no doubt, the expression: "You're pretty healthy!"† You believe, and rightly, that we Catholics refuse to admit that matters of faith can be contrary to reason. For the moment, this point is not of great importance. The great merit of your study is that it takes God out of abstract philosophy, and, by placing Him among our immediate, practical and contemporary realities, renews our contact with Him and renders Him natural.

For this reason, I make bold to tell you that your place is with Patmore, Péguy, Chesterton, and, if I dare say so, with myself, writers, all of us, whose task it is to restore a Catholic imagination and

† "De là sans doute, l'expression: Vous en avez une santé."

sensibility which have been withered and parched for four centuries, thanks to the triumph of a purely lay literature whose ultimate corruption we are witnessing today. What I also like in your latest work, and what seems to be something of an innovation with you, is a simple and candid tone, without any thought of being brilliant, a sort of detachment in face of a supremely interesting object, and a preoccupation to render your thought as lucid as possible, which sometimes produces very profound reflections, as, for one instance, when you speak of misfortunes which certain lives do not deserve but which they call down upon themselves. This is the point where talent becomes a virtue. How far you have come! And it does not seem the home stretch should be very far off now. We shall see, in the next number…!

Cordially,

P. C.

To Jacques Rivière
37 QUAI D'ANJOU, 6TH DECEMBER, 1912

My dear Rivière,

Heartiest congratulations on your last article. It is better even than the first. Your conclusion alone puzzles me a little, and I own I have had some trouble in understanding it. But I have no fears for you. You will end by escaping from narcissism and epicureanism, and from the hall of mirrors which shows a man nothing but a reflection of the images he projects on its walls.

Very affectionately,

P. Claudel

To Paul Claudel

PARIS, 2ND APRIL, 1913

My dear friend,

Forgive me for only thanking you today for your *Cantate.* I need hardly tell you what immense pleasure your gift gave me. First of all, because you were good enough to include me among those who received presentation copies. And also because I find your work admirably fresh and new. You have made certain rhythmical discoveries whose profundity amazes me. Throughout there is an astounding skill in movement, both simple and combined. In each and every phrase one would almost say that the words were forced to speak out by the sheer stress to which they have been subjected in order to give them their adjustment in the sentence. They inter-penetrate and form one solid mass as though under the pressure of an irresistible mechanism. And this is only one aspect of your work. There is, at the very same time, a sort of liberty, bordering on gratuitousness—something that is near neighbor to hesitancy and flexibility, which makes one somehow think of long grass in the wind. I cannot explain myself very well in a letter. I need to turn such things over and over in my mind. In any case, I feel no necessity to analyze my emotion in detail in order to be conscious that it is something very deep and never felt before.

I am just back from Bordeaux, where I spent a fortnight. I saw F——. We spoke a great deal about you and your *Cantate.* He is just as charmed with the book as myself.

I must stop, for I have other letters to write, far less pleasant, alas!

Sincerely your friend,

Jacques Rivière

To Jacques Rivière

57 QUAI D'ANJOU, PARIS, 4TH MAY, 1913†

Dear friend,

I am quite at ease on your account. I know that, some day or another, you will come to Jesus Christ. If there was any other alternative for you, you would know of it by this time. Here is the address you ask me for. Abbé Fontaine, vicar of Notre-Dame-Auxiliatrice, at Clichy. He is the priest who attended Huysmans in his last moments. He never speaks of that martyrdom and saintly death, which does so much credit to our own guild of writers, without emotion. For the past ten years he has been living in the midst of the terrible poverty that is only found on the outskirts of great cities.

Take the Nord-Sud to the Porte de Clichy, go along the Boulevard Victor-Hugo; after passing a cemetery, turn to the right, and at the end of about a quarter of a mile, you will see the chapel of Notre-Dame-Auxiliatrice, in a little side street. I have already given this address once before, to G——, who asked for it but never went. Good Heavens, why all this terror? Surely it is as simple a matter to go and consult a priest on the state of one's soul as a doctor on the state of one's health, or an architect about some alterations in one's house. Everything can be said in a perfectly calm, sensible and rational fashion.

† Jacques Rivière's own letters, written subsequent to this date, are unfortunately missing.

* * * * *

Goodbye! You are wrong to create terrors for yourself when what you have to do is so easy, simple and pleasant! Think of the comfort of finding yourself at home at last in a universe of justice and reason.

I would like Abbé Fontaine to read your two essays on *the Faith* before he sees you. Send them to him.

P. Claudel

To Jacques Rivière

FRANKFORT-ON MAIN, 22ND MAY, 1913

CENTENARY OF RICHARD WAGNER

Dear friend,

In thinking over the talk we had together the other day, I begin to have a few scruples. I am afraid I sought to present religion to you too much as a means to spiritual health and comfort; in a word, that I spoke to you only of its pleasantness and utility. These, after all, are secondary considerations, and rather sordid ones. The only reason we should believe in Jesus Christ is *because He is true.* God is not made for man, but man for God. Whether good or ill comes to ourselves from faith (though necessarily only eventual good can be the result) matters not a whit. In all fairness, I think I should make this point clear.

Do you know Jacques Maritain, a professor of philosophy at Stanislas, and who is a convert from protestantism? He seems to me a very distinguished thinker.

What marvels surround us at this moment! How interesting to see the grace of God, its natural channels intercepted by persecution, infiltrating directly, if one may use the word, into the natural man, and welling up, sudden and crystal-clear, in the most unexpected places! Only today I was told of the conversion of Psichari, Renan's grandson.

I read your article in the *N.R.F.*, and am awaiting the second part with a good deal of curiosity. Will you permit me a little criticism? It seems to me that you are so carried along by the interest of your idea, that occasionally you are not on your guard against dissonances. For example, I find this phrase: *en en enlevant tous les elements.* Please forgive me! I would not dare make such a remark with any other but myself.

Sincerely,

P. Claudel

To Jacques Rivière

FRANKFORT-ON-MAIN, 29TH MAY, 1913

My dear Rivière,

When you tell me that you have not the slightest idea what sin, remorse and contrition can mean, it is quite evident to me that you exaggerate. So vast a department of human nature cannot possibly be closed to you. Moral evil is as much a fact as physical evil; spiritual nausea is as real as nausea of the stomach, and, as you are neither an angel nor a scoundrel, I presume that you have not escaped its bitterness. We never reach the real core of our nature unless some overwhelming humiliation has driven us there, and until tears have welled from our hearts. It is not without good reason that tears are given the name of "the spring" and of *aquae scaturientis.* It is they which wash away the dead matter and debris of sin, whose accumulation poisons, atrophies and petrifies the soul and makes of it a dead thing. Tears and tears alone can unseal our eyes to the living light.

How is it possible that the thought, on the one hand of an eternal Life, of an eternal Beauty, of an eternal Love, of those grave and tender voices we hear in our hearts, and on the other hand, of our insatiable passions, our misery, our ingratitude, this wretched life of dust, turmoil and vanity, of the hell which is the wages of sin—*stipendium peccati,* and the other actual hell we see around us—how, I ask you, can all these, if we meditate upon them sufficiently, fail to give us some idea of our deplorable condition and of our dependence upon God's mercy? Such things are not idle imaginings. They are sensations as real and as desperately urgent as hunger or thirst. We cannot separate them from ourselves or regard them as so many knicknacks or curios without depriving them of their true value, and outraging and mutilating reality itself. How wretched and sordid an affair a reality would be in which nothing remained to desire and where the belly was left judge of all values!

In any case, remember that salvation has nothing to do with what one *feels*. Faith, an upright will, and a frank and sincere confession of our faults, are all that is asked.

When you speak of the cramping of your emotional nature which Christianity would entail, I hardly know what you mean. By sins, I presume you allude to the sins of the flesh. I can hardly suppose any tendency in you toward drunkenness, envy, violence, etc.

The first answer is that, if we become Christians, it is not for our personal pleasure or comfort, and that if God does us the honour to demand certain sacrifices, there is but one thing to do, and that is, to obey cheerfully.

The second answer is that, in the end, these sacrifices do not amount to very much. We are still living under the old Romantic idea that the supreme happiness, the main interest, the sole romance of existence, lies in our relations with women, and the sensual gratification we extract from these. One thing is overlooked, namely, that the soul and mind are realities too, just as strong, just as exacting as the flesh (they are really far more so!) and that, if we surrender to the latter what the former demands, it is to the detriment of other joys and other regions of beauty which will remain eternally closed to us. We empty a glass of bad wine in a salon or in a dive, and put out of our heads that virginal sea which is visible to others under the rosy morning sun.

Good is harder than evil: first, because it requires a *great* purity and sensibility of soul, which is only acquired by patience and interior recollection: secondly, because evil is a partial defect and good an adjustment of all our faculties. *Bonum ex integra causa, malum ex quocumque defecto.* But the horizons that goodness opens to us are incomparable ones, because goodness alone is in harmony with our reality, our nature, our life and our vocation. This is especially true where love is concerned. How absurd the romantic fumes of purely sensual love, and the bray of that great jackass Tristan, have always seemed to me! Human love never has any beauty except so long as satisfaction evades it. As for the delights of consummated love, the reason no artist has ever depicted them, is because they do not exist. A paradise which should consist in the total possession of a woman, body and soul, as an end in itself, does not seem to me to differ in any respect from hell. I am not speaking now of married love, which is something infinitely profounder and more beautiful. And I would add this. For a writer especially, there is no worse delusion than love. It is a career where he is absolutely certain, except at the price of becoming an imbecile, to be a failure.

Is this the sort of answer you expected from me? It is always harder to reach an understanding in matters of sentiment than where reasoning is involved. But, come! You pray, you go to Mass, you have made one loyal effort to confess. This is an enormous advance. From a certain point of view it is even heroic. And I am sure you will not want to stop now. By going on you can learn much more than I have ever been able to teach you.

Affectionately,

P. Claudel

To Jacques Rivière
HAMBURG, 5TH JANUARY, 1914

Yes, indeed, my dear friend, I am quite overjoyed.[†] Amid much that was bitter, one piece of good news, at least, reached me for this New Year. What you tell me takes away nothing from your merit or from the efficacy of the Sacrament you have received. Quite the reverse. You belong to the category of supra-sensible souls who always react into hardness and dryness. If you persevere courageously, if you are absolutely loyal, that seed of the Divine which ferments and swells in the heart of man will one day be felt in yours too. Don't worry your head about the little chamber of horrors and intimate grab-bag that you, like us all, carry round inside of you. From the moment that these loose parts are not turning any kind of machinery, and so long as these odds and ends are not influencing conduct, the thing has no significance whatsoever.

During the two months which have just come to an end, I have been keenly conscious of the incomparable—the unguessed-at marvel—that the love of God for us really is. My own despair comes from knowing myself so slack, so weak, so at the mercy of every stumbling-block.... God protect you, dear friend, you and your little child. What you have just done is so fine a thing!

As ever, affectionately yours,

P. Claudel

† In reply to Rivière's announcing that he had been to Communion on Christmas.

APPENDIX

~

Job, chapter XXX. "Lamentations of the Church in our own day."

(1) Quoniam sprevisti aquas Siloë quae vadunt in silentio.—*Isaiah.*

(2) Ostendisti populo tuo dura: potasti nos vino compunctionis.—*Psalm* LIX.

(3) Vide, Domine, et considera quia factus sum vilis.—*Lamentations of Jeremiah.*

(4) Vae vobis qui cogitatis inutile.—*Micaiah.*

(5) Tunc cognoscam, sicut et cognitus sum. (A cry from the abyss.)—I *Cor.* VIII, 12.

(6) Producam ergo ignem de medio tui qui comedat te.—*Ezechiel.*

Quotations sent by M. Claudel in Letter of 25th May (*see* p. 38).

(7) Et es eis quasi carmen musicum quod suavi dulcique sono canitur: et audiunt verba tua et non faciunt ea.—*Ezechiel.*

(8) Ego veni in nomine Patris mei et non accepistis me: si alius venerit in nomine suo, illum accipietis.—*John* V, 43.

(9) Pro eo quod *charitatem veritatis* non receperunt, ut salvi fierent, ideo mittet illis Deus operationem erroris ut credant mendacio.—II *Thessalonians.*

(10) Ubi est Deus qui fecit me, qui dedit carmina in nocte?—*Job.*

(11) Satiabor cum manifestabitur gloria tua.—*Psalms* XVI.

(12) Qui ventum observat non seminat, et qui considerat nubeis nunquam metet.—*Ecclesiastes.*

(13) Pater volo ut ubi Ego sum et illi sint mecum.—*John.*

Another word from the Abyss.

Ego sum—I am—Jahvé, the name of God itself.

(14) Gaude et laetare, filia Sion, quia ecce venio et habitabo in medio tui.—*Zacharias.*

(15) Absque muro habitabitur Jerusalem.—*Zacharias.*

(16) Secretum meum mihi, secretum meum mihi!—*Isaiah.*

(17) In circuitu impii ambulant.—*Psalm* XI.

(18) Quoniam humiliata est in terra anima nostra, conglutinatus est in terra venter noster. *Psalm* XLIII.

(19) Deserta facta est terra a facie irae agni, a facie irae columbae. —*Jeremiah.*

(20) Protegunt umbrae umbram ejus.—*Job.*

(21) Vinea mea coram me est.—*Canticle of Canticles.*

(22) Faith, Hope and Charity:

—*Credo, Domine, adjuva incredulitatem meam.*

—*Etiamsi occiderit me, sperabo in eum.*

—*Domine, compelle me amare te.*

Translation

(1) How hast Thou scattered the waters of Siloam, which flow in silence.

(2) Thou hast shown Thy people hard things: Thou hast made us drink the wine of sorrow.

(3) Look, Lord, and consider how vile I am made.

(4) Woe to you who devise that which is unprofitable.

(5) Then I shall know, even as I am known.

(6) I will bring forth a fire from the midst of thee to devour thee.

(7) And Thou art to them as a musical song which is sung with a sweet and agreeable voice: and they hear Thy words and do them not.

(8) I am come in the name of my Father and you receive me not: if another shall come in his own name him you will receive.

(9) Because they received not the love of the truth that they might be saved, therefore God shall send them the operation of error, to believe lying.

(10) Where is God who made us, who hath given us songs in the night?

(11) I shall be satisfied when Thy glory shall appear.

(12) He that observeth the wind shall not sow, and he that considereth the clouds shall never reap.

(13) Father, I would that where I am, they also may be.

(14) Sing praise and rejoice, O daughter of Sion, for behold, I am come and will dwell in the midst of thee.

(15) Jerusalem shall be inhabited as a town without walls.

(16) My secret to myself, my secret to myself (woe is me)!

(17) The wicked walk round about.

(18) For our soul is humbled down to the dust: our belly cleaveth to the earth.

(19) The earth is made desolate before the face of the wrath of the lamb—before the face of the anger of the dove.—

(20) The trees cover his shadow.

(21) My vine is before me.

(22)—I believe, O Lord! Help my unbelief!
—Even though He should slay me, I will believe in Him.
—Lord, compel me to love Thee!

Made in the USA
Middletown, DE
08 April 2024

52600628R00126